NESSIE

About the Author

Nick Redfern is the author of more than thirty books on the worlds of the paranormal, the supernatural, and the unknown. His previous titles include *Chupacabra Road Trip*, *Monster Diary*, *There's Something in the Woods*, and *Monster Files*. Nick has appeared on dozens of television shows, including SyFy Channel's *Proof Positive*, History Channel's *Monster Quest*, Nat Geo Wild's *The Monster Project*, and Fox News. Nick lives just a short drive from Dallas, Texas's infamous Grassy Knoll. He can be contacted at his blog, World of Whatever: http://nickredfernfortean.blogspot.com.

Exploring the Supernatural Origins
of the Loch Ness Monster

NICK REDFERN

Llewellyn Publications
Woodbury, Minnesota

FIRST EDITION
First Printing, 2016

Cover design: Kevin R. Brown
Cover illustration: Dominick Finelle, The July Group
Interior photographs on pages 3, 41, 106, and 193 © Colin Stott; photographs on
    pages 71 and 84 are public domain

Llewellyn Publications is a registered trademark of Llewellyn Worldwide Ltd.

Library of Congress Cataloging-in-Publication Data
Names: Redfern, Nicholas.
Title: Nessie : exploring the supernatural origins of the Loch Ness Monster /
    Nick Redfern.
Description: First edition. | Woodbury, Minnesota : Llewellyn Publications,
    [2016] | Includes bibliographical references.
Identifiers: LCCN 2016017114 (print) | LCCN 2016018519 (ebook) | ISBN
    9780738747101 | ISBN 9780738750071 ()
Subjects: LCSH: Loch Ness monster. | Monsters—Scotland.
Classification: LCC QL89.2.L6 R43 2016 (print) | LCC QL89.2.L6 (ebook) |
    DDC 001.944—dc23
LC record available at https://lccn.loc.gov/2016017114

Llewellyn Publications
A Division of Llewellyn Worldwide Ltd.
2143 Wooddale Drive
Woodbury, MN 55125-2989
www.llewellyn.com

Printed in the United States of America

Other Books by Nick Redfern

Chupacabra Road Trip
There's Something in the Woods
Monster Diary
Monster Files
The Bigfoot Book

Forthcoming Books by Nick Redfern

Shapeshifters

Contents

Acknowledgments

A very big "thank you!" goes out to all of the following: Everyone at Llewellyn Worldwide Ltd., and particularly Amy Glaser, Kat Sanborn, Sandy Sullivan, Kevin Brown, and Donna Burch-Brown; my literary agent, Lisa Hagan, for her hard work, enthusiasm, and friendship; and Colin Stott, for generously giving me permission to reproduce a number of his Loch Ness–themed photos in this book.

Introduction

The Loch Ness Monster: just about everyone has heard of it. A large number of people claim to have seen the long-necked, humped leviathan of the deep. Some have even photographed and filmed it. "Nessie," as the beast is affectionately known, has been a staple part of the world of the unexplained since 1933, when the phenomenon of the monster exploded in spectacular, planet-wide fashion. Since then, millions of people have flocked to the shores of the 22.5 mile long and 744 foot deep loch, all in the hopes of seeing the elusive creature. Attempts have been made to seek out Nessie with sonar equipment, aircraft, balloons, and even submarines.

Theories abound as to what Nessie is—or, far more likely and correctly, what the Nessies are. Certainly the most captivating theory, and the one that the Scottish Tourist Board, moviemakers, and the general public find most appealing, is that which suggests the monsters are surviving pockets of plesiosaurs. These are marine reptiles that the domain of zoology assures us became extinct tens of millions of years ago. The possibility that the monsters are actually giant-sized salamanders holds sway in more than a few quarters. As does the idea that perhaps massive eels are the culprits. Then there are scenarios involving sturgeon, oversized turtles, and catfish, and even crocodiles, giant frogs, and hippopotami!

Numerous Nessie enthusiasts, investigators, and authors have spent years—*decades*, in some cases—pursuing their quarry. They have done so in a fashion that uncannily mirrors the obsessive actions of the fictional Captain Ahab, in Herman Melville's acclaimed 1851 novel *Moby-Dick; or, The Whale*. But it's all, and *always*, to no avail. No matter the number of days, hours, weeks, and years spent, and no matter just how advanced the technology utilized to find the animals might be, it forever ends in failure. After more than eighty years of intensive investigation, the Nessies still evade capture, discovery, or classification. Is this all down to sheer bad luck and inept investigations? Certainly not. Rather, it's a case of people looking for the answers in the completely wrong direction.

Over the decades, numerous books have been written on Nessie. For the most part, they all follow the same path. It's a path that is becoming more and more weary, predictable, repetitive, and worn as the years go by. Those same books typically take a near-identical approach: they chronicle the most famous sightings, the chief players in the saga, and the theories that exist to explain the monster—and then they leave it at that. All of which brings me to the theme of the book you are now reading.

For me to simply regurgitate all the same old stories at length, and to uphold the same old theories for what the beasts of that massive loch might be, would be pointless. Such a thing has now been done to the point of utter tediousness. And doing so has achieved nothing meaningful, in any way whatsoever. It's time for a fresh approach to solving the mystery. It's an approach that takes us down terrifying, paranormal, and occult pathways and leads us into a dark realm inhabited by Nessies that are far removed from the flesh-and-blood creatures that so many people believe, want, or assume them to be. As my book shows, there is demonstrable evidence that the monsters of Loch Ness are of a definitively supernatural—rather than a flesh-and-blood—nature.

In the pages that follow, you will learn how, from even the very first sighting of the Nessies ever recorded, the phenomenon became steeped in the world of supernatural high-strangeness. Magical rituals, satanic rites, necromancy, dragon-worshiping cults that engage in bloody sacrifice under a full moon, bizarre synchronicities, UFO sightings, encounters with the dreaded Men in Black, and even exorcisms are part and parcel of the phenomenon that has become known as the Loch Ness Monster. As are the creature's connections to one of the world's most infamous occultists, to curses, to magicians, and even to a wide range of *other* strange creatures that *also* call Loch Ness their home.

Loch Ness, Scotland: the home of monsters

Not only that; one would imagine that most people would love to catch sight of a Nessie. And they probably do—at least, until they actually see it. Then it's a very different kettle of fish. It's a curious and intriguing fact that many witnesses react not with amazement, incredulity, or excitement. No, the response to encountering a Nessie—and particularly so up-close and personal—is very often an acutely different one. People talk of the beast being "an abomination," "something abnormal," "a loathsome sight," and "something which still haunts us." Others have commented that after seeing the creature, "we were all sick." That they felt "appalled." That "my dog ... lie[s] crouching and shivering." One said: "I never wish to see the like of it again." There is, then, something decidedly *wrong* about the Loch Ness creatures; something which provokes reactions far beyond those one might expect—even when encountering something fantastic and unknown.

Without doubt, strange and sinister things lurk in the deep and turbulent waters of Scotland's most famous loch—and have done so for centuries upon centuries, maybe for even longer. But here's the important factor: they are not what you may have assumed they are. They just might be the most nightmarish and malignant things you could possibly ever imagine.

There can be no doubt that the tales of the creatures of Loch Ness have caught people's attention on a truly massive scale. That same attention, however, is provoked not just by the tales of the monsters but by the loch itself, too. To say that Loch Ness has an air and atmosphere of mystery and intrigue about it is an understatement. The gigantic loch is steeped in legend, folklore, mythology, and history.

It lies along a huge fault line called the Great Glen Fault, the origins of which date back literally hundreds of millions of years. The fault runs through the similarly named Great Glen, which includes

Loch Ness, Loch Lochy, Loch Oich, Loch Linnhe, the River Ness, and the River Lochie. Loch Ness is home to a near-magical-looking thirteenth-century structure called Urquhart Castle, which would not look at all out of place in the next *Lord of the Rings* movie. The ruined castle's large, stone Grant Tower overlooks the mysterious and dark waters of the loch, just as it has for centuries. It provides an excellent view of the deep, mysterious waters that harbor something brooding and abominable. The ancient history of the castle is dominated by warfare, death, and tribal confrontations.

Cherry Island—a man-made slab of land on Loch Ness—was, in the fifteenth century, the domain of a now long-gone castle. When the castle went, so did its legends and lore. A now submerged island nearby, *Eilean Nan Con* in the Gaelic language—and which translates to "Dog Island" in English—was the home of vicious packs of hunting hounds. Quaint and largely unchanging old villages and hamlets surround the huge body of water. The ways and beliefs of times long gone still persist amongst the locals. Thick and expansive woods surround the loch, provoking wonder and awe at what secrets they might hide. Huge, green slopes dominate the entirety of the loch. And as for those waters that hold so many monstrous secrets, they contain more freshwater than every other lake in Wales and England *combined*. No wonder, then, that Loch Ness has a reputation for being a lair of beasts.

So, with that all said, come with me now as we take a trek into the dark and turbulent domain of Nessie, the world's most supernatural monster.

1

Nessie: In the Beginning

It is highly ironic—considering the many attempts that have been made by monster hunters to suggest the Nessies are plesiosaurs, salamanders, or giant eels—that even the very first reported encounter with one of the creatures of Loch Ness was steeped in occult mystery. It's a certain St. Adomnán of Iona we have to thank for bringing this intriguing case to our attention. The story can be found in Book II, Chapter XXVII, of St. Adomnán's *Vita Columbae*. To say that it's quite a tale is, at the very least, an understatement. Born in the town of Raphoe, Ireland, in 624 AD, St. Adomnán spent much of his life on the Scottish island of Iona, where he served as an abbot, spreading the word of the Christian God and moving in very influential and power-filled circles. He could count amongst his friends King Aldfrith of Northumbria and Fínsnechta Fledach mac Dúnchada, the High King of Ireland. And he, St. Adomnán, made a notable contribution to the world of a certain famous lake monster.

St. Adomnán's *Vita Columbae* (in English, *Life of Columba*) is a fascinating Gaelic chronicle of the life of St. Columba. Columba was a sixth-century abbot, also of Ireland, who spent much of his life trying to convert the Iron Age Picts to Christianity, and who, like Adomnán, was an abbot of Iona. In 563, Columba sailed to

Scotland, and two years later happened to visit Loch Ness—while traveling with a number of comrades to meet with King Brude of the Picts. It turned out to be an amazing and notable experience, as *Vita Columbae* most assuredly demonstrates.

Slaughtered by the monster

Adomnán began his story of St. Columba's visit thus:

"... when the blessed man was staying for some days in the province of the Picts, he found it necessary to cross the river Ness; and, when he came to the bank thereof, he sees some of the inhabitants burying a poor unfortunate little fellow, whom, as those who were burying him themselves reported, some water monster had a little before snatched at as he was swimming, and bitten with a most savage bite, and whose hapless corpse some men who came in a boat to give assistance, though too late, caught hold of by putting out hooks."

If the words of Adomnán are not exaggeration or distortion, then not only was this particular case the earliest on record, it's also one of the very few reports we have in which one of the creatures violently attacked and killed a human being. Adomnán continued his account by saying that St. Columba ordered one of his colleagues—a man named Lugne Mocumin—to take to the River Ness, swim across it, pick up a boat attached to a cable on the opposite bank, and bring it back. Mocumin did as St. Columba requested: he took to the cold waters. Or, more correctly, to the lair of the deadly beasts.

Evidently, the monster was far from satisfied with taking the life of just one poor soul. As Mocumin swam the river, a terrible thing ominously rose to the surface, with an ear-splitting roar and with its huge mouth open wide. St. Columba's party was thrown into a state of collective fear as the monster quickly headed in the direction of Mocumin, who suddenly found himself swimming for his very life. Fortunately, the legendary saint was able to save the day—and save Mocumin, too. He quickly raised his arms into the air, made a cross out of them, called on the power of God to help, and thundered at the monster to leave Mocumin alone and be gone. Amazingly, the monster did exactly that.

Invoking God apparently had quite an adverse effect upon the Nessie, something which the pages of *Vita Columbae* makes very clear. Immediately after St. Columba made the sign of the cross and called on the supernatural power of God to save Mocumin, the creature fled for safety and vanished below the surface. This was very good news for Mocumin, who was barely ten feet away from the monster when it decided to cease its attack. The amazed group fell to their knees, praising God for having saved their friend. Even what St. Adomnán referred to as the local "barbarous heathens" were impressed by the astonishing spectacle of the monster being denied a second victim.

One could quite easily make a rational case that the story was simply a parable, a fable; perhaps one designed to demonstrate the power of the word of God over the domain of evil. After all, St. Columba, as noted above, spent years trying to convert the Picts to Christianity, so what better way than to suggest that God had the power to repel deadly Scottish lake monsters? On the other hand, however, it's decidedly intriguing and curious that of all the large bodies of water in Scotland that the story could have been set in, it turned out to be none other than Loch Ness—which just happens to be the home of a creature of the deep. Or, to be totally accurate, it was the River Ness, an approximately twelve-mile-long body of water that flows out of the loch's northern end.

A little-known fact in this story is that this was not the only close encounter St. Columba had with a Nessie. St. Adomnán told of how one of the creatures allegedly, and incredibly, towed the saint's boat—a currach, a wooden vessel coated in animal skins and which was much-used by the Celts of that era—across the loch, which led Columba to give the monster its freedom in the loch. A variant on this story suggests that Columba confronted the beast in the waters near Urquhart Castle—which, rather notably, is a hot spot for Nessie sightings today and has been for many decades.

From a monster to a spectral ship

It's worth noting that the paranormal issues surrounding the Loch Ness monsters and St. Columba and his boat do not end there. None other than the ghostly form of St. Columba's ancient currach has been seen traveling on the expansive waters, and on more than a few occasions, too. Just two years into the twentieth century, the supernatural currach was seen by one Finlay Frazer, a resident of Strathenick. Colin Campbell, the brother of Alex Campbell—a man who played a major role in the development of the Loch Ness Monster controversy, as we shall later see—had a close encounter with the spectral craft during the Second World War. And a man named Thomas O'Connell saw its spectral shape in 1962, near Invermoriston.

Colin Campbell said of his extraordinary and eerie sighting that it was a dark night when, quite out of the blue, he saw at a distance of around ninety feet a stationary boat on Loch Ness. It was, however, no ordinary boat. It lacked any illumination itself, but was bathed in an eerie, mysterious, white-blue glow. Campbell was sure that what he saw was the spectral form of an ancient, primitive craft constructed millennia earlier. From the very outset, then, the saga of Nessie—and those that were exposed to it almost fifteen hundred years ago—was absolutely steeped in matters of a paranormal nature. And it still is.

Dragons on the loose

The next report of a Nessie dates from around nine hundred years later, specifically, in the early sixteenth century: 1520. It should be stressed this does not mean there was a complete absence of encounters in the intervening years. It suggests that, possibly, no one chose to speak about what they may have seen. Or, more likely, if the details of sightings were passed down orally, and amongst close-knit communities close to the loch, they may have become forgotten and lost to the fog of time.

As for the 1520 case, the details came from a man named David Murray Rose, a historian, genealogist, and respected antiquarian who was particularly active from the late 1800s to the 1930s. It was in 1933, when Nessie mania was in full swing, that Rose contacted the *Scotsman* newspaper about his knowledge of an early episode of the Nessie variety. In a letter of October 20, 1933, Rose stated that post-St. Columba, the next reference to the presence of strange creatures in Loch Ness harked back to 1520. He cited as his source an old manuscript that was filled with tales of all manner of strange and legendary creatures, such as fire-breathing dragons and ghostly hell-hounds. According to Rose's research, the book in question described how one Fraser of Glenvackie slaughtered just such a dragon—in fact, what was said to be the very last Scottish dragon—but not before the beast managed to scorch much of the landscape. Interestingly, Rose said that the author of the book made a comment to the effect that although the dragon was slain, the creature of Loch Ness lived on.

While Rose's account is unfortunately brief, it does demonstrate that more than five hundred years ago there existed a tradition of monstrous animals in Loch Ness, long before the term "Nessie" was coined.

It should also be noted that although we have an absence of reports of strange, serpent-like creatures from Loch Ness between the sixth and sixteenth centuries, that's certainly not the case in other parts of Scotland. Given that—as we shall later see—there have been more than a few reports of the Nessies exiting the water and moving on land, there's a possibility of a tie-in between the following early saga and the unknown things that dwell in Loch Ness, which is why I make specific mention of it.

A monster-worm on the rampage

Our world has no shortage of modern-day monsters. The world of the past had no shortage, either, as the strange saga of what became known as the Linton Worm makes very clear. A tale that dates back to the 1100s, it tells of a horrific, man-eating, giant, worm-like beast that terrified the good folk of Linton, Roxburghshire, which is located on the Southern Uplands of Scotland. According to the old tales, the Linton Worm was somewhere between ten and twelve feet in length, which, if true, effectively rules out any known British animal—wild or domestic—as being the culprit.

Rather oddly, so the old legend went, the huge worm had two homes. In part, it lived in the heart of Linton Loch—a small, boggy area and the ideal place for a monster to hide. Its other dark abode was Linton Hill, which even today is referred to as Worm's Den, such is the enduring nature of the legend. That the beast apparently had the ability to leave the water and slither across the landscape of Scotland is a matter that is integral to the story of the Loch Ness Monster. That will become very clear, and very soon.

The beast's reign of terror

By all accounts, the worm was a creature best avoided at all costs: cows, sheep, pigs, and even people were all food for the monster.

Quite naturally, the people of Linton were thrown into a collective state of fear when the slithering thing decided to target their little village. People became petrified to leave their homes, lest they became the next victims of the marauding beast. Doors and windows remained locked. Farmers stayed home. Children were kept indoors. That is, until a man named John de Somerville came upon the scene.

When told of the nature of the monster that had brought terror to Linton, de Somerville—known as the Laird of Lariston—had a local blacksmith create for him a razor-sharp spear, which he, de Somerville, intended to use to slay the mighty beast. Fortunately, he did exactly that, by setting the spear aflame and plunging it into the throat of the monster after seeking it out at Worm's Den. The frightful beast fought back, its wormy form writhing, turning, and twisting violently atop the hill, but it was all to no avail. Exhausted, and on the verge of death, the beast retreated to its labyrinthine lair within Linton Hill. It was neither seen nor heard of again.

The Linton folk never forgot the valiant act of John de Somerville, and a sculpture commemorating de Somerville's brave deed was created in Linton Church, as William Henderson noted in his 1879 book, *Notes on the Folk-Lore of the Northern Counties of England and the Borders*. He pointed out, correctly, that the sculpture shows a helmeted knight atop his steed, doing battle, and with his lance firmly implanted in the throat of a monster. The knight, however, is not fighting just one beast in the sculpture, but two. Is it possible that there was not just one worm of Linton but possibly a pair of them? Or, maybe, even more? It's an intriguing theory to muse upon. Today, both the church and the effigy remain intact—and still provoke wonder, and perhaps even a little fear, in those that visit the little village of Linton.

Moving on, there is another deadly beast that was on the loose centuries ago, and which may also have been of the same breed as the Nessies.

The wyvern of Wales

An approximately one-mile-long body of water in Clwyd, North Wales, Llyn Cynwch Lake is renowned for a story of its resident monster, a wyvern—a story that dates back centuries, although the precise date is admittedly unknown. Within ancient legend, the wyvern was very much a dragon-like animal, one to be avoided at all costs. Reptilian, and sporting large and membranous wings of a bat-like appearance, it stood on two powerful legs and had a powerful tail that it used to sting and kill its prey, not unlike a scorpion. In some cases, and just like the dragon of old, the wyvern was said to occasionally breathe fire. All of which brings us to the monster of Llyn Cynwch Lake.

For as long as anyone could remember, the lake and its surrounding landscape made for a peaceful and relaxing environment. But that all changed when a deadly wyvern decided to swoop down on the lake and make its home there. Tranquility, there was no more. The creature was undeniably monstrous. It was described by fear-filled locals as looking like a huge, coiling, and writhing monster with a humped back and an undulating neck. On its back were two wings, and its feet displayed razor-sharp claws of the kind that could likely tear a person to pieces. Its breath was reportedly poisonous and green in color. In no time at all, the Welsh wyvern began to eat its way through the local populations of sheep, cattle, and pigs. Terrified village folk stayed behind locked doors after the sun set, which was when the beast typically surfaced from the waters of the lake. The time came, however, when enough was well and truly enough. Something had to be done to combat the beast.

Doing battle with the beast

A local warlock—known as the Wizard of Ganllwid—believed that he stood a good chance of slaying the deadly monster. As he knew, all previous attempts to kill the animal had failed—as a result of its noxious breath causing instant death to anyone and everyone close enough to be exposed to it. So, the wizard had a brainwave: he decided to round up a team of archers who could shoot the wyvern from a safe distance. It was all to no avail. It was as if the beast had a sixth-sense about it, and whenever the bowmen were around, the wyvern would stay steadfastly below the surface of the water.

Finally, there was a breakthrough, one which proved to be the turning point in the tumultuous affair. On one particular morning, a bright and sunny one, the wyvern left the waters of the lake and slithered its way onto the shore, where it proceeded to bask under a hot sun—something which the monsters of Loch Ness have been seen doing on more than a few occasions. As luck would have it, a young shepherd boy, named Meredydd, happened to be in the area and saw the beast, asleep, as he was directing his sheep to his father's farm.

Fortunately, the monster was deep in its slumber—as was evidenced by its hideous, skin-crawling snoring, which was more like the hiss of a gigantic snake. Its body moved rhythmically, its strange form glistening like wet leather. Realizing this was quite possibly the one time, more than any other, that the wyvern could be killed, Meredydd raced to nearby Cymmer Abbey and breathlessly told the monks of what he had just seen. He asked for a much-revered axe that hung in the abbey, suggesting that if anything could kill the wyvern it was surely the axe, which allegedly possessed magical powers. The monks quickly agreed and in mere minutes Meredydd was heading back to Cynwch Lake, for a battle to the death. But of whose death, exactly, Meredydd was not so sure. Nevertheless, he was determined to do his very best to rid the area of the loathsome beast.

Fortunately, as Meredydd got back to the spot where the abomination lay, he could see that it had not moved; it was still sleeping. There was no time to lose. The young shepherd boy used all his might to raise the axe over his head and then brought it down hard and fast on the neck of the monster. In a spilt second, the head was severed from the neck. The jaws of the severed head snapped wildly and widely, in a fashion akin to that of a headless chicken, while the neck thrashed around for a few moments before falling limp on the grass. The nightmare was over—no thanks to a powerful warlock, but all thanks to a young shepherd-hand.

And let's not forget the paranormal aspects of the story: the magical axe, the presence of a wizard, and the wyvern's deadly breath. Again, we see a lake monster associated with matters magical and mystical. Now it's time to look in-depth at the way in which the saga of the monsters of Loch Ness developed post-St. Columba. It's a tale of supernatural terror and mysterious mayhem.

2

The Rise of the Kelpies

The most important aspect of the saga of St. Columba is that which suggests an unfortunate soul was violently slaughtered by a Loch Ness Monster. As for why it's so important, the answer is as intriguing as it is disturbing. Within the folklore of Loch Ness and much of Scotland, there are centuries-old legends and myths concerning supernatural, violent, shapeshifting creatures known as kelpies. Or, in English, water-horses. It should be noted, though, that although the creatures are assumed to be one and the same, there is one noticeable difference between the tales that specifically refer to kelpies and those that talk about water-horses. Typically, water-horses are far more at home in deep, sprawling lakes, while kelpies prefer pools, rivers, marshes, and lakes of a particularly compact kind. Then there is a variant of the kelpie known as the Each-Uisge, which is a far more murderous monster than the kelpie, but which is clearly of the same supernatural stock.

The term "kelpie" has unclear origins, although the most likely explanation is that it is a distortion of the Gaelic *calpa*, which translates as "heifer." Kelpies are terrifying, murderous creatures that lurk in the depths of Scottish lochs, canals, and rivers—and more than a few of them in Loch Ness. Not only that, but like werewolves, kelpies are definitive shapeshifters, creatures that can take on multiple guises including hideous serpentine monsters, horses, hair-covered humanoids, beautiful maidens of the mermaid variety, and horse-like creatures. The kelpie is solely driven by a crazed goal to drown the unwary by enticing and dragging them into the depths, killing them in the process.

While numerous old bodies of water in Scotland have kelpie legends attached to them, it's surely no coincidence that the bulk of the legends are focused upon Loch Ness. And, as we'll see later, there is good evidence to suggest that the creatures of the loch do indeed have the ability to change their form and morph and mutate into numerous states. It's also notable that many reports of the Loch Ness Monsters suggest they have mane-like hair flowing down the back of their head and neck—not unlike the mane of a horse, which may well have prompted both the name and imagery of the water-horse. But before we get to the matter of Loch Ness, let's take a deeper look at this malevolent, demonic entity, the kelpie of darkest Scotland.

Stay away from the water

Reports of, and legends pertaining to, strange creatures in the large lochs of Scotland date back centuries—specifically to the sixth century, as we have seen with the St. Columba affair of 565 AD. With hindsight, they sound very much like kelpies, even though they had acutely different names and titles. For example, in 1900, folklorist Alexander Carmichael told of a beast known as the Glaistic. It was a hideous monstrosity. Half-human and half-goat, it dwelled in isolated bodies of water, always ready to pounce on and slaughter the unwary and the unfortunate.

Moving on, we have the Lavellan, described by some as a shrew-like animal and by others as a lizard-style beast. Both its saliva and breath were said to be deadly—to both man and beast.

Note that the reference to the Lavellan having deadly breath echoes the old story of the wyvern of North Wales's Llyn Cynwch Lake. Loch Tummel, in Perthshire, Scotland, has its own kelpie, even though it too goes by another name, the Buarach-Bhaoi. Highland Perthshire Tourism says of this fearsome thing that it resembled nothing less than a gigantic leech and typically wrapped itself around horses and then dragged them into the depths of its underwater abode—draining the unfortunate animals of blood in definitive vampire style.

Loch Lindie was the deadly domain of Madge, a violent, murderous monster that, said Edward Nicholson in 1897, had the power to morph into numerous forms, including those of a raven, a cow, a horse, and a hare. Similarly, Loch Leathan was the lair of the deadly Boobrie, yet another body-altering thing with nothing but cold-hearted killing on its crazed mind.

Lakes of death

So far as can be determined, it was in the late 1700s that those words, "kelpies" and "water-horses," first appeared in print. It's a story that has its origins in the 1740s, however. That was when a renowned poet, William Collins, who died while still in his thirties, made mention of the kelpie in one of his many odes. It was not until 1788, however, that Collins's poem was published, through the agency of Alexander Carlyle, as *An Ode on the Popular Superstitions of the Highlands of Scotland.*

Eighteenth-century records demonstrate there was some degree of disagreement regarding whether kelpies lived within the deep waters of lakes like Loch Ness or if they lurked at their very edges, in shallow, marshy waters, and possibly even on the land. This in itself is worth noting, since there have been more than a few sightings of the Nessies being seen near the shore, basking, lying on the shore itself, and even lurking in the surrounding woods, as strange as such a thing might sound. This suggests a collective body of data, and an enduring and attendant tradition, of the kelpies being creatures that chiefly lurked in the water, but that on occasion moved about the landscape—which is exactly what we have been told about the Nessies since the early 1930s.

While, as I mentioned earlier, the kelpie can take on the guise of numerous animals, there is no doubt that the horse-like kelpie is the one most often reported. And, generally, a black horse. The downfall of the unwary traveler occurs when he or she, generally late at night, is walking past some large expanse of water. Suddenly, just such a horse appears out of the darkness and seems to beckon the victim, in inviting fashion, to climb onto its back. That so many ill-fated people did exactly that suggests they were under some form of supernatural spell. This echoes the Middle Ages–era tales of shapeshifting fairies that could place people into a state of being pisky-led, meaning that their minds were enslaved and their actions dictated and controlled by the magic of the wee folk. Perhaps, and in view of the shapeshifting abilities of both, the fairies and the kelpies of old were actually one and the same.

When the entranced person mounts the horse, the tranquil atmosphere changes immediately—and in terrifying fashion. The infernal beast charges into the water, plunging into its depths and dragging its victim to his or her violent death. On other occasions, the kelpie will take on the form of a beautiful woman, who also invites people to walk to the water with her—shades of centuries-old stories of men becoming hypnotized by the visions of voluptuous fairy-queens in ancient English woods. And, vice-versa, the kelpie will appear as a dashing young man, as a means to capture and drown young women.

In 1807, a poet named James Hogg, who deeply studied the folklore and legend of Scotland, said that somewhat similar to the kelpie was the water-cow. It dwelled in the allegedly bottomless St. Mary's Loch, a three-mile-long body of water located in what are termed the Scottish Borders. Although nowhere near as dangerous as the kelpie, the water-cow could also transform itself into multiple forms and was best avoided at all costs; largely as a result of its penchant for enticing people to walk to the shore, and then violently dragging them into the water and killing them by drowning.

A perfect example of this enticing aspect of the kelpie's manipulative character and powers comes from Christian Isobel Johnstone. With her husband, an Edinburgh, Scotland, printer named John Johnstone, she ran the *Edinburgh Weekly Magazine*. In 1815, she told a chilling story of how, one day some years earlier, a group of young boys decided to go swimming in a particularly wild and dark loch; it was situated on a mountain, in the vicinity of Glen Ogle. In no time at all, a powerful-looking white horse rose from the depths and swam to the shore. On reaching land, the horse stretched itself out, as if beckoning the boys to climb on its back. Feeling adventurous—as young boys do—they did exactly that. It was not just a big mistake. It was also the last mistake any and all of them would ever make. When the young friends were atop the horse, it suddenly reared up and shot into the lake, drowning them as it speedily propelled itself below the surface and into the inky depths.

A monster in multiple guises

On other occasions, the kelpie will manifest not as a horse, but as something akin to a hair-covered wild man; or, one might be justified in saying, a Bigfoot. This latter description is absolutely personified by an 1879 encounter at Bridge 39 on England's old Shropshire Union Canal—at which, late one January night, a man and his horse were attacked by a crazed half-human, half-ape-like animal that leapt out of the shadowy surrounding woods. Shaggy and covered in hair, it became known as the Man-Monkey. Very notably, local police associated the presence of the creature with the then-recent death of a local man, one who was drowned in the canal under mysterious circumstances. It's clear from a study of the affair that the locals, and even the police, incredibly, believed the man in question was dragged to his death in the waters of the canal by something akin to an English equivalent of a Scottish kelpie.

As the kelpies became both more prevalent and reported, so did their presence in popular culture. The renowned poet Robert Burns said in "Address to the Devil" in 1786:

When thowes dissolve the snawy hoord
An' float the jinglin icy-boord
Then water-kelpies haunt the foord
   By your direction
An' nighted trav'lers are allur'd
   To their destruction.

Despite its supernatural, malignant powers, the kelpie was not a creature of indestructible proportions. If one knew its weaknesses, one could defeat it. It's fascinating to note that one of the primary ways that a kelpie could be killed was with silver, and particularly with a silver bullet. Most people will, of course, be familiar with the legends that a silver bullet is the one thing, more than any other, guaranteed to put down the world's most famous shapeshifting monster of all time, the werewolf. There is a vampire parallel, too:

kelpies had deep aversions to Celtic crosses. And let's not forget that the vampire is a shapeshifting creature also, having the ability to morph into various forms, including a bat and a wolf. All of which brings us to the matter of the kelpies of Loch Ness—a lake which, as studies have shown and as will now be revealed, has more kelpie legends attached to it than any other Scottish loch.

3

Water-Horses in Loch Ness

Roland Watson is one of the most respected figures in the fields of Nessie and kelpie lore and history, someone who has spent an enormous amount of time tracking down just about each and every legend and tale of the kelpie. His sterling work has led to the discovery of accounts suggesting that, at one time or another, no less than fifty Scottish lochs had kelpie traditions attached to them. One might find this too incredible for words, until one realizes there are numerous lochs and smaller lochans, as they are known, in Scotland. In that sense, the argument cannot be made that wherever bodies of water existed in Scotland, the locals regularly applied kelpie legends to them. The exact opposite is actually the case: it was only certain select lochs in which the kelpies lurked and viciously hunted humans.

Far more revealingly, Watson's study of pre-1933 publications, books, and manuscripts that mention kelpies in Scottish lochs shows that a full 43.6 percent of all the reports cited came from none other than Loch Ness. Again, we see evidence of a tradition of monsters in Loch Ness, and long before the media furor of the 1930s could ever have been contemplated or anticipated. Watson's work also shows that there once existed a lore of such water-horses in lochs very close to Loch Ness: Lochs Lundie, Bruiach, Laide,

Corrie Mohr, and Meiklie. A strong indicator, perhaps, that on occasion the Nessies took to the land and traveled to nearby smaller lochs—possibly then returning, under cover of darkness, to their much larger, regular abode.

Watson's work does not stand alone. There is a great deal more evidence of kelpie activity in pre-twentieth-century times at Loch Ness.

Prophecies and disaster

Those within the skeptical camp very often take the approach that since it was not until 1933 that the saga of the Loch Ness Monster began in spectacular fashion, the whole thing is nothing but a relatively modern-day myth. Those same skeptics, however, so very often conveniently forget to mention the fact that the mystery *didn't* actually begin in 1933 after all. Or, perhaps, the presumed forgetfulness of the skeptics is actually a deliberate ploy to avoid dealing with what the rest of us commonly refer to as facts. Theirs is a wholly erroneous and lazy assumption.

We have already addressed the sixth-century affair of St. Columba and the 1520 account uncovered by David Murray Rose. Add to that the tales of the water-horses, the kelpies, and the Each-Uisge, and the statistics collected by Roland Watson, and we see ample evidence of high-strangeness afoot in Loch Ness—and in other Scottish lochs, too—long before the sensational events of 1933 began.

Just one example is that of January, 1849, when, according to Watson's research, the *Aberdeen Journal* reported that a veritable deluge of rain had caused the River Ness to catastrophically burst its banks. It was something which led the turbulent, churning waters to collapse three bridges in the area, one of them being the Ness Bridge. The newspaper noted that there were several prophecies concerning the old bridge, one being that it was not destined to fall until it found itself under attack from what was described as the whale-like beast that lurked in Loch Ness.

As this story shows, in the 1840s tales of monsters at Loch Ness were well known and discussed.

Mistaking monsters

A further perfect case in point is an incident—a very strange one—that occurred at Loch Ness in the summer of 1852. Just one day into July of that year, the *Inverness Courier* newspaper reported on something notable that occurred during the previous week. According to the account, on the day in question the loch was still and calm and bathed in tranquility. For a while. It wasn't long before the people of Lochend were plunged into states of excitement by the sight of what seemed to be a pair of animals swimming in Loch Ness. Those same two animals appeared to be heading for the northern edge, from the opposite side of Auldourie. And such was the commotion, we are told, the entire neighborhood rushed out to see what all of the fuss was about.

There was a great deal of excited debate among the locals as to what the creatures were. The theories, said the media, ranged from nothing less than sea serpents traversing the waters to a pair of whales. Or perhaps even a couple of seals, which do frequent the loch on occasion. The people of Lochend were taking no chances, however. The men armed themselves with hatchets said to resemble centuries-old battle-axes, the younger men and boys grabbed scythes, and the women pitchforks. They were ready to do battle with the monsters of the mysterious deep.

As the animals got closer to the shore, however, there was a collective sigh of relief when one of the throng declared them nothing stranger than a pair of deer. As it transpires, he was wrong.

But they weren't monsters, either. When the creatures got much closer, one and all realized that what they were seeing were not deadly water-horses but a couple of ponies that, opined the *Inverness Courier*, were taking a swim to cool down, given that the day in question was a particularly hot one.

Although the affair was demonstrated to be nothing untoward or hair-raising in nature, it's highly instructive and revealing for several important reasons. Note that the journalist who penned the article observed that when the ponies were first seen—at a distance—there was talk of them being something along the lines of sea serpents. This clearly demonstrates a *pre-existing* mid-nineteenth-century knowledge and acceptance of fantastic serpentine beasts in Loch Ness. One cannot be in fear of kelpies in Loch Ness without there being a history of sightings of such things in the loch in the first place. Finally, that all of the village folk armed themselves to the teeth with makeshift weapons is a strong indication that the people of that era and area knew, full well, that the loch was filled with strange creatures that, on occasion, turned hostile. In that sense, from this case of mistaken identity we can learn and interpret a great deal about beliefs in *real* monsters in Loch Ness. Much the same can be said of something that happened around a decade later.

Loch Ness is "full of them"

In 1862, Scottish scholar John Francis Campbell told the story of what he intriguingly termed the Water-Bulls of Loch Ness. Based on what the people of Loch Ness had told him, Campbell said the creatures were paranormal amphibians that had the ability to physically change themselves into multiple, varied forms, including bison, buffaloes, and walruses. They were, then, shapeshifters of a kelpie type. It's very revealing that Campbell said Loch Ness was, and I quote, "full of them."

Moving on, it's now time to take a look at the curious saga of Nessie and the necromancer, a twisting tale of terror that blends monsters and magic into one heady brew.

4

The Weird World
of Willox the Warlock

To understand the sheer extent to which the kelpie and its deadly actions impacted the people who lived in the direct vicinity of Loch Ness in the nineteenth century, one only has to look at the life of a legendary character who called Loch Ness his home. His name was Gregor "Willox" MacGregor, although he was more famously known as Willox the Warlock—and not without a great deal of justification, either. Such was the level of renown that surrounded Willox, when he died in 1833 the *Inverness Courier* newspaper devoted significant page space to his obituary. Indeed, it was far less an obituary and far more like a nineteenth-century equivalent of a page on Wikipedia. The October 16, 1833 article—titled "Death of a Warlock"—began:

"On the 5th instant, were deposited in their last abode in the Churchyard of Kirkmichael, Strathtown, the mortal remains of Gregor MacGregor, alias Willox, whose name, if not his person, have been long and extensively known in the Northern Counties as 'Willox the Warlock.' Gregor was the last of a line of ancestors, long the object of awe and veneration, as the possessors of the only means ever known of prying into futurity, and of controlling and circumventing the works of both natural and supernatural agents!"

Willox gained both renown and respect when he became one of the very few people to take on a kelpie in battle at Loch Ness and come out of the confrontation as the victor. It's interesting to note that although skeptics and debunkers claim there is no pre-1933 lore of monsters in Loch Ness, the Inverness Courier's article of 1833 openly noted that monstrous kelpies lurked on the banks of both Loch Ness and Loch Spynie, with the specific, deadly intent of capturing and killing those who unwisely crossed their paths.

It was when the kelpie of Loch Ness tried to make Willox the Warlock its next victim that the beast finally met its match.

A confrontation with a deadly monster

Late one night, Willox was walking along "a wild and solitary pass on the road between Strathspey and Inverness," as per W. Grant Stewart in The Popular Superstitions and Festive Amusements of the Highlanders of Scotland. It was a walk Willox would never forget. As the darkness hung all around him, the deadly kelpie loomed into view in the guise of an inviting horse. According to the old tale, the kelpie in question sported a piece of yellow metal that resembled the bit of a horse's bridle, as a means to try and further emphasize its deceptive horse-themed imagery. The supernatural thing was apparently confident that Willox would mount the horse, thus forever sealing his fate when it dragged him, screaming for his life, beneath the waters of Loch Ness.

Not so. Astutely realizing that he was not in the presence of a friendly horse on a late-night wander around the shores of Loch Ness, but instead a murderous lake monster in disguise, Willox wasted no time in whipping out his claymore—an old-time, two-handed longsword. He brought it down hard and fast on the kelpie's nose, which badly damaged the creature's jaw and brought it to its knees. The bridle was sliced in two pieces and Willox quickly grabbed the aforementioned piece of yellow metal.

It was at that point, incredibly, that the kelpie did something very strange. Instead of launching an attack on Willox, it ... *spoke to him.* Clearly realizing that it was up against a formidable foe, the kelpie suggested that if Willox was to return the bridle, it would be on its way and the bloody confrontation could be forgotten. Fully aware that nothing which came out of the mouth of a deceptive and deadly kelpie should be considered the gospel truth, Willox not only refused to return the bit, but also made it very clear to the monster of Loch Ness what he thought of it. The beast reacted in apologetic fashion, even though this was very likely yet another carefully thought-out ruse on its part.

Supernatural entities and second sight

As Willox had zero goodness in him for the supernatural fiend of the loch, instead of returning the bit, he demanded to know the secrets of the beast's paranormal powers. Perhaps realizing that it had to appease the man if it stood any chance of having its priceless bit returned, the monster agreed to reveal the truth of its uncanny abilities. It said that were it not for the fact that Willox had broken its bridle, it would likely have killed him in bone-breaking fashion; but now that Willox had the upper-hand, the kelpie revealed the amazing secret of the bridle. By looking through the holes in the bit, the monster said, it would be possible for Willox to encounter a wealth of Loch Ness–based supernatural entities, ones which were rarely ever seen by mortal man, such as devils and fairies. The bridle would also give Willox the power of second sight.

Willox, now fully confident that he definitely had the upper hand, poked fun at the kelpie, stating he regretted to inform it that he had no intention of returning the bit. Instead, said Willox, he intended to use it for his own purposes, such as learning how to call forth those same supernatural entities to which the kelpie referred, and to employ the bit's powers of second sight. The shocked monster—who had believed that revealing the powers of the bit to Willox would actually make him fearful of the bit rather than embrace it—demanded that the bit be returned. Willox's only response was to make a hasty bid, across the darkened pass, for the safety of his home. The kelpie was far from being done, however. It followed Willox, doing its best to try and convince him to return the bit—still in polite but obviously deceptive tones.

Eventually, however, the creature's true, horrific nature was finally revealed. It became enraged, to a near-homicidal degree, and lunged at Willox. Fortunately, it was to no avail; Willox's claymore sword disarmed the monster and made it as meek as a mouse. The kelpie, nevertheless, continued to closely follow Willox to the latter's home, quietly imploring him to return the bit. Willox, however, stood his ground and flatly refused. As a last act of desperation, the monster charged at Willox's home, which he shared with his wife, and slammed into the front door, ready to do battle for the bit.

Willox raced to the rear of the old stone house. He threw the bit through an open window, directly into his wife's waiting, eager hands, and then charged back to the front door. Willox had a very good reason for ensuring that the bit was inside the house rather than outside: the front door was adorned with a rowan cross, which the kelpie was unable to pass. Realizing that it had been outwitted and bettered by Willox's knowledge of the occult, and with the man himself menacingly swinging his sword in its face, the hate-filled monster screamed and swore at Willox, its frustration and anger clearly evident.

The violent confrontation was over and Willox was now a man possessed of magical powers. His reputation as a warlock, as a purveyor of magical arts, and as someone who knew how to command the secrets of second sight was sealed. It ensured that he quickly gained a reputation in the area as a powerful and mysterious necromancer. It should be noted, though, that despite the somewhat dark and disturbing atmosphere that surrounded Willox the sorcerer, he stressed until his dying day that there was nothing negative or sinister in his character or conduct.

Should we take every aspect of the legend of Willox the Warlock literally? Those who believe the animals of Loch Ness to be of a flesh-and-blood nature would most assuredly say no. Those who conclude that the Nessies are nothing more than the products of misidentification, hoaxing, and mischief-making would also say no; although for very different reasons, obviously. If today's Loch Ness Monsters and the kelpies of centuries past are one and the same, however, and they have supernatural origins, all bets are wide open. The mysterious world of the occult. The dark domain of the necromancer. The actions of those supernatural entities that hovered around Loch Ness and which Willox was warned about. They may yet all hold hideous secrets of a kind that we can scarcely begin to comprehend.

The high-strangeness that dominated nineteenth-century-era Loch Ness doesn't end there, however.

5

Further Reports of the Early Kind

In early October 1868, what was described as a large fish was washed up on the shores of Loch Ness, approximately two miles west of Lochend Inn. The discovery of the remains of the animal led huge crowds of people to descend on the loch, all eager and excited to see what had fallen into their hands, so to speak. The discovery proved to be overwhelmingly anticlimactic, however. The giant fish was actually nothing but a six-foot-long bottle-nosed whale. How it got there was a mystery—at least, it was a mystery until it was discovered that a crew of fishermen had caught the animal in the ocean. They had relieved it of its valuable blubber and then dumped it on the shore of Loch Ness for all to see, and with the intent to cause amazement, surprise, and maybe even a not-insignificant amount of fear.

But, as with the 1852 saga of the misidentified ponies, the case of the dead bottle-nosed whale reveals a good deal of intriguing data. Once again the *Inverness Courier* was quick to report on the discovery. The unnamed reporter who covered the story said that the finding of the animal reminded local folk of a large fish of a similar appearance that had been encountered, on many occasions and for many years, in Loch Ness.

So, despite the events of 1868 being the result of nothing stranger than a good-natured hoax, they prompted talk of sightings of *other* large, unknown animals in the loch from years earlier; specifically, in a time frame when talk of the much-feared kelpie was all-dominating. Also, that the fishermen specifically chose Loch Ness for the site of their prank suggests they, too, knew of the old stories of monsters inhabiting the loch. After all, they could have chosen just about any of the many and varied Scottish lochs for their joke. That they specifically chose Loch Ness is eye-opening and speaks volumes in relation to what they knew of the pre-existing supernatural lore of the loch. It was surely not down to mere chance.

One more thing on this particular matter: when the body of the whale was found, and before it was identified, the media reported that the whole affair boded nothing but negativity, famine, and disaster for the people of Loch Ness. Again, this implies a longstanding acceptance of the supernatural nature of the monsters, and even their abilities to curse the people of the area and to blight the landscape.

An early land-based encounter

Moving on to 1880, there is the sensational saga of one E. H. Bright. On the day in question, along with a friend, and when he was just eight years old, Bright was strolling along the shore of Loch Ness in the vicinity of Drumnadrochit, as the story goes in *The Leviathans*. It wasn't long before something astounding happened. Bright had an encounter with a Nessie not in the water, but on the land. The beast, apparently, loomed out of the camouflage of an area of dense woodland, which was located at a distance of around three hundred feet from Bright and his astonished pal.

To say that the animal was a weird one is an understatement of epic proportions. It was described as being elephant-like in both size and color, had a long neck, and possessed a very small head that was somewhat akin to a snake's head in terms of its shape. And it moved in a very strange fashion: an awkward waddle that suggested it was not at all accustomed to, or built for, moving across the wild, hilly, wooded landscape of rugged Scotland. As it reached the water, the beast plunged into its depths with an almighty splash and was gone from view in seconds.

Bright and his friend, by now understandably scared out of their wits, raced to the home of Bright's grandfather and, in stressed-out fashion, told the old man of what they had just seen. At first he tried to play things down, possibly to try and calm the two boys, and made a joke about them having maybe indulged in a couple of shots of good old Scottish whiskey. Later on, however, and after a set of strange, large, three-toed tracks were found near the shore, Bright's grandfather quietly admitted to him that tales of strange creatures in Loch Ness extended well into the history of the area, but that everyone knew it was wise to stay silent on the matter. Don't forget, too, that the kelpie—although predominantly a beast of water—was known for leaving the deep waters and lurking in the shallows, the marshes, and even on land. In view of that, we might be wise to suggest that E. H. Bright and his friend were very lucky not to have been pulled down into the depths of Loch Ness by a murderous, land-roaming kelpie.

The view from a graveyard

Around this very same time, another, similar event occurred. The origins of the story are somewhat convoluted, but certainly not unbelievable given all that we have seen so far. This tale, likewise described in *The Leviathans*, came from an Edward Smith, who got the story from an elderly lady who, with her two brothers, saw a Nessie when she and they were children, at some point around 1879 or 1880. It may not be irrelevant to note that when the three saw the monster, they were sitting on the slopes that overlook an old graveyard, one which stands at the site of Aldourie Castle. After all, what more appropriate a place for a murderous kelpie to lurk could there be than the domain of the dead? As they ate their lunch among the old graves, the trio heard strange and unearthly noises coming from behind them. Turning around quickly, they were terrified out of their wits by the sight of a full-blown monster in their midst. According to the woman, the beast was larger than an elephant, had a thin, long neck, and moved in a side-to-side fashion. For a brief period it peered at the three children, and then it waddled off to the loch and vanished into its murky waters.

A kelpie and a giant frog

The year 1880 witnessed one of the most spectacular and nerve-jangling of all Nessie encounters, described years later in the *Northern Chronicle*. The unlucky eyewitness—and that really is the only way we can describe him—was a man named Duncan Mac-Donald. It was his task to take a dip into Loch Ness, at Johnnies Point, and examine a ship that had sunk in the entrance to the Caledonian Canal at Fort Augustus. MacDonald was confronted by something far stranger than a sunken ship. After being lowered to a depth of around thirty feet, he suddenly raced for the surface, practically screaming to his friends to haul him aboard their vessel.

It was several days before MacDonald could bring himself to confide in the rest of the crew what he had seen. It was nothing less than a frog-like creature, perched on a rock shelf, and which was around the size of a fully-grown goat. The beady-eyed monster and the terrified diver even locked eyes on each other, until MacDonald, momentarily paralyzed with fear, managed to swim for safety and reached the surface. Thankfully, the monster-sized frog—or whatever it was—did not pursue him, and there was no repeat of the deadly attack involving St. Columba hundreds of years earlier.

A lair of supernatural beasts

There is also the admittedly scant story told to Nessie investigator and BBC newsreader Nicholas Witchell. According to one Jock Forbes, a gypsy woman told of seeing a terrible beast lying in a stretch of bracken near the Loch Ness shore at some point in the 1890s. Since hoaxes tend to be elaborately weaved affairs, the very brief data in this case is actually supportive of its reality.

The "demon-steed" of Loch Ness

Then, just seven years before the end of the nineteenth century, James Mackinlay revealed something very noteworthy in his book *Folklore of Scottish Lochs and Springs*. He said, "A noted demon-steed once inhabited Loch Ness, and was a cause of terror to the inhabitants of the neighborhood. Like other kelpies, he was in the habit of browsing along the roadside, all bridled and saddled, as if waiting for someone to mount him. When any unwary traveler did so, the kelpy [sic] took to his heels, and presently plunged into deep water with his victim on his back."

The cases cited in this chapter are not, by a long stretch of the imagination, the totality of nineteenth-century reports of weird animals seen in, and on the land immediately around, Loch Ness. In fact, the exact opposite holds true. They are, however, some of the more revealing and amazing cases on record and which demonstrate undeniable beliefs in kelpies and supernatural animals at the loch. When collectively placed under one banner, they make it abundantly clear that the Nessies were known to the village folk and townfolk of the region, and long before the mania of the twentieth century ever began.

Time-travel at the loch?

One of the strangest stories of paranormal weirdness at Loch Ness comes from an acclaimed author on all manner of mysteries, Andrew Collins. As Christmas 1979 loomed, Collins—with colleagues Graham Phillips (a parapsychologist) and Martin Keatman (a UFO investigator)—spent a week in Scotland investigating the Nessie enigma. It involved interviewing witnesses, spending time poring over old archives in Inverness's library, and checking out the loch itself. It was while they were deep in the heart of their investigation that the trio uncovered a very weird story. Back in the early eighteenth century, a young couple inexplicably vanished while riding a horse and trap near Loch End, on the south shores of Loch Ness. Rumors circulated that the pair was either murdered or abducted. And neither the horse nor the trap were ever seen again.

It would have remained a complete mystery were it not for one thing; a very uncanny thing. More than one hundred years later, and at the height of a tumultuous thunderstorm, a young man and woman walked into a local almshouse, inquiring if the priest that oversaw it would give them shelter for the night, which he did. The priest couldn't fail to see that the pair were dressed in the kind of clothing that had been popular around a century or so earlier. Plus, the two seemed very confused, dazed, and bewildered, and completely unable to explain where they were from. They remained in that odd, altered state for a couple of days, after which they simply walked out of the almshouse and were never seen again. When the story got out, several of the locals recalled old tales of the events of a century earlier, and the missing pair of young lovers.

Was this, perhaps, a case of a slip in time having occurred? Did the couple vanish from the eighteenth century only to briefly and incredibly manifest in the nineteenth? Possibly, yes. That the fantastic event should have occurred at Loch Ness is yet another example of how infinitely peculiar the entire area is.

Now it's time for us to take a look at another great beast of Loch Ness. It's one who arrived on the scene, in controversial fashion, at the very end of the nineteenth century, and who did nothing but add to the air of supernatural malevolence that hung over Loch Ness like the sword of Damocles.

6

The Greatest Beast of All

Born in the English county of Warwickshire on October 12, 1875, Edward Alexander Crowley is far better known, today, by his much more infamous and near-legendary moniker "Aleister Crowley." Aleister was a hedonist, bisexual, drug addict, and astrologer. He was also someone who amusingly provoked outrage amongst closed minds everywhere and became known as the "Wickedest Man in the World." As he was brought up in a strict Christian household, one that allowed no room for questioning religious teachings, it was practically inevitable that Crowley would exhibit a significant amount of teenage rebellion. Although he entered the highly respectable Trinity College, Cambridge, in 1895, it wasn't long before young Aleister was on the lookout for new pursuits, adventures, and wild times. It was also during this period he took on another name: "The Great Beast, 666." In 1898 he became a member of the Hermetic Order of the Golden Dawn (which practiced occult rituals to achieve personal and spiritual development of the highest level and contact with divine supernatural entities), and by 1900 he was a fully-fledged 33rd degree Mason.

Then, in 1904, Crowley established the school of Thelema, the ethics and teachings of which he spelled out in the pages of *The Book of the Law*. "Do what thou wilt shall be the whole of the law" and "Love is the law, love under will" were the two prime directives adhered to by Thelemites everywhere. Such could only be achieved by adhering to the teachings of magickal ritual and rite. It's notable that the writing of *The Book of the Law* took place while Crowley was honeymooning with his wife, Rose, in Cairo, Egypt. It was indeed a magickal time. Crowley did his best to summon up into our reality various elemental spirits. Rose, meanwhile, channeled messages concerning the falcon-headed Egyptian god Horus. It was, then, quite the alternative way in which to celebrate one's marriage! But not for Crowley: for him the extraordinary was the norm, as was living life to the full, giving his body and soul to what many might call the dark side and provoking outrage and shock just about everywhere he went. And that just happened to include Loch Ness.

A house of horror

It's important to note it was not random chance which, in 1899, took Aleister Crowley to Loch Ness. The location was as important as the purpose he had in mind. In some respects, it was even *more* important. Crowley's goal was to perform what he termed the great Operation of the Sacred Magick of Abramelin the Mage. And to successfully perform it meant finding an abode that perfectly fit the requirements of the ritual, namely one that was situated in an isolated spot. Since Crowley had specific and highly complex needs, I have presented for you, below, his very own words on this matter. They demonstrate exactly how much work went into finding what ultimately turned out to be a place called Boleskine House. Before we get to Crowley's words, however, a brief bit of background on the old manor house is required.

Built on the southeast side of Loch Ness in the late 1700s by Archibald Fraser, Boleskine House was originally intended to be a hunting lodge. And, for many years, that is exactly what it was. It stands over both the B852 loch-side road and an old graveyard, one which, ever since the house was built, has had a reputation for being a place of evil and of supernatural malignancy. The house, not far from the villages of Foyers and Inverfarigaig, is even *connected* to the graveyard by an old tunnel, one that is rumored to have been used by witches and warlocks in centuries long gone. Not only that, but locals maintain that the house, constructed in the eighteenth century, stood upon the site of an old church that caught fire, leading to the deaths of the entire congregation, who were deep in prayer when the fire broke out. Reportedly trapped, they were all roasted alive. All of which brings us back to Crowley. Of his ideal place to conduct those grand rituals, he said in his 1922 book, *The Confessions of Aleister Crowley*:

"There should be a door opening to the north from the room of which you make your oratory. Outside this door, you construct a terrace covered with fine river sand. This ends in a 'lodge' where the spirits may congregate. It would appear the simplest thing in the world for a man with forty thousand pounds, who is ready to spend every penny of it on the achievement of his purpose, to find a suitable house in a very few weeks. But a magical house is as hard to find as a magical book to publish. I scoured the county in vain."

That is until he found a certain old house at a certain creepy Scottish loch. Interestingly, on coming across Boleskine House, Crowley felt an instant connection to it—and a full-blown supernatural connection, no less. He was of the feeling that Boleskine House operated, in effect, as a portal or doorway through which supernatural entities and secrets could be channeled. It is unclear to what extent Crowley, while in residence, had an awareness of the long tradition of kelpies in Loch Ness. It should be noted, however, that he had at least *some* knowledge of the controversy. For example, he had certainly heard of—and even wrote about—magical water nymphs in Loch Ness. And, when all is said and done, a water nymph is a perfect title for a shapeshifting beast of the deep.

Malevolent spirits at Crowley's abode

Crowley, who stated that Boleskine House fulfilled all of his needs, decided to begin his magical exercise at Easter, and commenced with the construction of a terrace and a lodge, something which, in total, took around six months to complete. Due to certain supernatural hazards the exercise might provoke, he invited a colleague to share the experience with him. The man in question was Charles Rosher, like Crowley a member of the Golden Dawn and a friend to Crowley's teacher, Allan Bennett. Rosher intended to stay with Crowley for months. He ended up leaving—or, rather, *fleeing*—inside of no more than three weeks. The reason: the presence of unseen evil forces that Rosher was sure had descended upon Boleskine House and which were intent on making his life a living hell. Such was the nature of Rosher's hasty and terrified exit that Crowley knew nothing of it until his butler informed him his friend was gone. The two did not see each other again for years.

If something supernatural and evil had descended on Boleskine House and Loch Ness, then it didn't take long before it began affecting and infecting the people that lived around the loch. On one occasion, shortly after moving into Boleskine House, Crowley returned to the abode after a stroll in the hills only to find a priest sitting in his, Crowley's, study. As pale as a ghost and deeply worried, the priest confided in Crowley that the keeper of the lodgehouse, a man named Hugh Gillies, who was described as being a lifelong teetotaler, had been drunk for days and even tried to murder his own family.

Things got worse. An old friend of Crowley's from Cambridge visited—and, like Charles Rosher, intended to stay for a lengthy period of time. He didn't succeed either. The friend was gone in less than two weeks after displaying panic-attack-type symptoms and telling Crowley, in fear-filled tones, that Boleskine House was filled with terrible, malevolent spirits.

Crowley himself acknowledged the claims of a bleak and eerie atmosphere. He specifically chose to work in the one room that, more than any other, offered a fair degree of sunlight—and which was in stark contrast to the rest of the house. Even in that particular room, though, he was forced to introduce artificial lighting, such was its bleak and shadowy atmosphere. It turns out that around this time, Crowley had a falling-out with various individuals in the Order, and so he took himself off to Mexico for a while, where he had adventurous times, scaling peaks with English mountain-climber Oscar Johannes Ludwig Eckenstein. Nevertheless, the magnet-like lure of Loch Ness and Boleskine House drew "the Great Beast" back to Scotland, and he continued with his studies and plans. He got married, too.

Rage, dementia, and tragedy

"I shall always feel a little grateful to Boleskine for giving me my wife," said Crowley in his *Confessions*. He was talking of his beloved, Rose Edith Kelly, whom he wed in 1903. "Although in later years," he revealed, "this union which held so much for both of us whilst it lasted became a domestic tragedy."

It was after their travels around Egypt that Crowley and Rose returned to Boleskine House. Things did not go well. A "rival magician" surfaced, Samuel Liddell MacGregor Mathers, a founder of the Hermetic Order of the Golden Dawn. Crowley believed that Mathers caused his entire pack of bloodhounds to die under mysterious, supernatural circumstances. His servants began to fall ill, with all manner of ailments. Then, worst of all, on one particular morning, Crowley heard wild, hysterical screaming and cursing coming from the kitchen. A workman had become inexplicably rage-filled and attacked Rose. Such was the frenzied and ferocious state the man had been plunged into, Crowley and his staff were forced to lock the deranged man in the coal-cellar and await the arrival of the local police.

Rose fortunately recovered, but there was still more tragedy to come. In 1911, Crowley was forced to have Rose committed to an asylum, as a result of the onset of dementia which had been provoked by her out-of-control alcoholism. Crowley left Boleskine House forever two years later, in 1913. Twenty years later, however, when Nessie fever exploded here, there, and everywhere, Crowley proved to be very vocal on the matter of the monster.

All will soon be revealed. Until then, let us focus on the matter of the Nessies in a brand-new century.

7

A New Century Dawns

Alexander MacDonald made mention of Scottish lake monsters in his 1914 book, *Story and Song from Loch Ness-side*. He said: "The fairy-lover in this story is identified in many parts of the Highlands with the water-kelpie, of which the conception that prevailed generally was one that inspired repulsiveness. There seems no getting away from the fact that the idea represented some sort of monster that, in the far back, obscure corridors of the past, came across the path of man as he slowly but diligently was making his way upward and onward."

Four years later, Cyril H. Dieckhoff, a monk at Fort Augustus Abbey, opined that even though much of what was written about the kelpie was clearly folkloric in nature, the beasts had a basis in fact. It was his firm belief that the tales were specifically born out of a combination of inherited memory and oral lore of giant, violent creatures of an unknown kind that had lived during the earliest years in which the Celts first appeared on the scene. It's hardly surprising, then, that when the Nessie phenomenon hit the headlines in 1933, Dieckhoff became a fervent follower of the mystery and an adherent of the theory that Loch Ness was the home of terrible monsters.

Loch Ness to Loch Latch

In February 1934, the *Scotsman* newspaper ran an account of a sighting of one of the Nessies at the turn of the twentieth century—possibly between 1902 and 1904, the witness having been admittedly unclear on the precise time. The *Scotsman* had actually picked up the tale from the Canadian press, which had run the story of a man who had lived in Inverness thirty years earlier, but by 1934 had moved to live in St. Thomas, Ontario. According to the man, as a young boy he had been told of a sea serpent that dwelled in the waters of Loch Latch, which is located above Loch Ness. As a child, he had gone on a fishing trip to Loch Latch with an equally young friend. While there, they heard that a local farmer and minister, and two visiting businessmen from Inverness, had caught sight of an unknown animal's long neck and serpent-style head as they stood chatting on the shore just a few days previously. Not surprisingly, the two boys—although adventurous and excited by the tale—were reluctant to head out to the water and plunder gulls' nests of their eggs. They were almost certainly in fear of being dragged down to their deaths by the monster. Given the very close proximity between Loch Latch and Loch Ness, one has to wonder, again, if under cover of darkness one or more creatures had stealthily migrated from one locale to the other, and back again.

A traumatic encounter and Crowley's ball lightning

In 1930, a full three years before the term "Loch Ness Monster" was created and became forever famous, a fascinating account surfaced from a man named Seton Gordon. In his book A *Highland Year*, Gordon told his readers of how, just a couple of years before the start of the First World War began (which would have been around 1912 or 1913, since the war began in 1914), a man who lived in the direct vicinity of Loch Ness was enjoying a summer's day by taking his small boat out on the waters. He ended up wishing he had done nothing of the sort. According to Gordon, the man raced for the safety of the shore. When questioned by his friends what was wrong, the fear-filled man said that while he didn't expect anyone to believe him, he had encountered a beastly thing looming out of the water. He refused to describe its appearance beyond stating that he earnestly hoped he would never encounter it again.

It's also worth noting that in the 1910s none other than Aleister Crowley had a very weird experience at a large expanse of water. It wasn't at Loch Ness, however. It was in the United States, at Newfound Lake in New Hampshire. The year was 1916, on what was very appropriately a dark and stormy night. At the time, Crowley was hunkered down in a small old cottage on the shores of the lake when he encountered something highly unusual. He described seeing, to his amazement, a brightly lit ball of fire, close to a foot in diameter and bobbing in the air, just to the right of his right leg. Suddenly, as Crowley looked on in amazement, the fiery ball exploded, provoking a slight electric shock to his right hand.

What Crowley described sounds very much like a rare atmospheric phenomenon called ball lightning, which has been described in *Scientific American* as "a luminous sphere, most often the size of a small child's head" which "appears usually during thunderstorms, sometimes within a few seconds of lightning but sometimes without apparent connection to a lightning bolt. ... Its lifetime varies widely, ranging from a few seconds to several minutes; the average duration is about 25 seconds." There have also been tales of the ball exploding, which sometimes has lethal repercussions.

It's interesting to note that ball lightning is also associated with earthquakes. And why should that be so interesting? Well, because Loch Ness itself is on a fault line; the fault runs from the southwest to the northeast and provokes around three quakes per year at the loch. That there have been a number of encounters with ball lightning at Loch Ness over the years may well be explainable by that same seismic activity. It's most odd, however, that Loch Ness's most infamous resident (next to the Nessies, of course), Aleister Crowley, should have had an encounter with this very same rare and poorly understood phenomenon at yet another lake, thousands of miles away.

As the twentieth century progressed, so did encounters with the Loch Ness Monsters. All of which brings us to the time in which the creepy phenomenon became world-famous: the 1930s.

8

The Loch Ness Monster
is Born

Despite the undeniably large body of lore, dating back centuries upon centuries, of strange supernatural animals—kelpies—living in Loch Ness, there is no doubt that it was not until 1933 that the phenomenon of Nessie caught the attention of the general public and the media. And not just in Scotland, but all across the world, too. Many researchers of the Loch Ness controversy who are doubtful that the stories have merit make much of the fact that, until the 1930s, things were relatively tame on the monster front. They use this as ammunition to suggest that Nessie is a product specifically of the twentieth century, one designed to titillate tourists, boost Scotland's revenue, and ensure media attention for the area. This is an outrageous and disingenuous approach to take, for two specific reasons. First, as we have seen, legends of the animals date back more than 1,500 years. Second, there is a very simple reason why the Nessie phenomenon didn't take off—as in, stratospherically—until the 1930s. And it has nothing whatsoever to do with tourism, hoaxing, or the press.

Prior to 1933, there was only one road that permitted travel around the loch, despite the gargantuan size of that famous body of water. It was the General Wade's Road, constructed way back in 1715, which went from Inverness to Fort Augustus. That was it. Nothing else. At all. Plus, much of the road ran through the surrounding hills, thus obscuring a good, close view of the loch. In addition, even where the road came close to the water, it did so in some of the more heavily wooded and forested areas. This, too, meant that a good view of Loch Ness was barely available—anywhere. For all of these reasons, it's no wonder that the Nessies only attracted the attentions of the locals. And let's remember that many of those same locals were extremely reluctant to say too much to outsiders about their encounters with the monsters.

That all began to change, and massively so, in 1932. That was the year that marked the start of construction on a brand-new road, one which would run along the length of the loch's north shore. What makes this road so significant in the story of Nessie is that it provided the average car driver, truck driver, and motor-cyclist with a practically wide-open view of the loch along its entire length. And, most important of all, *for the very first time, ever.* Finally, those driving by Loch Ness could see its massive watery expanses—and, as history has graphically shown, more than a few monsters, too. As all of this demonstrates, there is nothing whatsoever suspicious about the sudden increase in Nessie sightings in 1933—regardless of what the skeptics and the debunkers might wish us to believe.

Disturbing the beasts from their slumber

There is something else that may have provoked more and more monster sightings in the early 1930s. During the course of constructing the new road, the workmen involved had to resort to a great deal of blasting to create a route amid the dense, stony environment. That the massive, and very loud, explosions may have disturbed the beasts—and prompted them to surface more often than usual to see what on earth was afoot—is a theory that many Nessie seekers adhere to. It's certainly not out of the question: locals spoke of deafening booms and almighty bangs, and of massive chunks of rock hurtling into the air and coming crashing down into the waters of Loch Ness.

Keeping this in mind: it's interesting to note that in February 1932, when the new road was in the early stages of construction, a local mailman saw in the loch something strange, which he described as looking like a boat, albeit an upturned one. The man, James Cameron, was sure that whatever the thing was that he encountered at Shrone Point, it was a living but unknown animal. Perhaps it was a Nessie, concerned and curious about all the burgeoning new commotion.

Monster mayhem on the roads

Although 1933 was certainly the year that birthed Nessie, one year earlier there was a very strange occurrence at Loch Ness; one that is very often overlooked or ignored. The reason why, you will see, is very easy to fathom—it is at extreme odds, in terms of the description of the creature, with other reports. It does not, therefore, sit well with many Nessie investigators. Too bad! High-strangeness is at the very heart of this book, which ensures that this case gets the airing it richly deserves. The witness was a Lieutenant McP Fordyce and the date was April 1932, two months after James Cameron's sighting at Shrone Point.

At the time, Fordyce was living in the English county of Kent, but, along with his fiancée, he had traveled by car to Aberdeen, Scotland, to attend a family wedding. Given that the drive there was such a long one, instead of simply driving immediately all the way back home, Fordyce decided to show his fiancée a bit of his homeland. The young lovers had a late evening: a romantic dinner, a stroll through the town, an encounter with a band of men playing bagpipes. It was a perfect slice of ancient Scottish tradition, one that Fordyce's girl would never forget. There was soon to be something else she would never forget, and neither would Fordyce.

The camel-horse freak of the woods

On the following morning, the pair decided to hit the road running and hopefully make the journey back to Kent in good time. It was a bright and sunny day for the drive; a drive which took them past Loch Ness as far as Foyers, at which point they turned onto the road to Fort William, away from the loch side and into the heart of the wooded areas that dominate certain portions of the loch. According to Fordyce's memory of the event, he was driving at around twenty-five miles per hour when he and his fiancée were shocked and amazed by the sight of a large animal appearing from the dense woods and then making its way across the road, at a distance of around 450 feet. He added that the beast moved like an elephant, but appeared to be something akin to a strange combination of a camel and a horse, even to it having a camel-like hump on its back and a small head positioned on a long neck. Displaying welcome gumption, the adventurous Fordyce stopped the car, jumped out, and decided to pursue the monster on foot. As he got closer, still keeping a respectful distance—just in case the creature turned violent—he could see that the rear of the animal was gray in color and had wild and shaggy hair, while its long neck reminded him very much of the trunk of an elephant.

Unfortunately, and surely to the consternation of monster-seekers everywhere, Fordyce had left his camera in the car. He then realized the somewhat precarious position he was in—

stalking a large and unknown animal in the woods—and decided that pursuing the thing was perhaps not such a good idea after all. A worm-slaying armored knight of old, Fordyce was most definitely not. By his own admission, he and his fiancée spoke about the amazing event for the entire journey back home. The only theory they could come up with was that the animal had escaped from a zoo. He admitted he was sure that such a large creature would easily be seen by others and quickly caught. Yet as history has shown, the Nessies remain as elusive today as they were back in 1932, when Fordyce's one-in-a-million chance encounter occurred.

Aside from confiding in family members, Fordyce stayed silent on his sighting until 1990, when, as an old man, he contacted the media and his story became public knowledge. His description of the beast as camel-like and even hairy is, admittedly, at odds with many other reports, as was his observation that it had an elephantine gait. The latter comment suggests that the creature walked on legs rather than moved around using flipper-like appendages, which are so very often reported in Nessie encounters. Whatever it was that Fordyce encountered, it remains practically unique in terms of its physical appearance. Of course, if the Nessies are shapeshifting kelpies that can take on multiple forms and guises, then the strange appearance of the animal is not quite so strange after all. In fact, it would be exactly what one would expect.

The wave of encounters in 1933 prompted a Miss K. MacDonald to come forward with her account of a strange-looking creature in Loch Ness, one which looked *nothing* like the classic humped, long-necked monster that was all the rage. But it didn't resemble Fordyce's monster, either. According to Miss MacDonald, she saw a six-to-eight-foot-long animal swimming the River Ness, approaching the Holm Mills weir. She described it, bizarrely, as looking somewhat crocodile-like, and added that it seemed to have very large teeth—or possibly even elephant-like tusks!

Welcome to the Loch Ness Monster

The date on which history was *really* made—as the newspapers and the public saw it, anyway—was April 14, 1933, although admittedly the facts didn't surface until May 2. The latter was the date when a man named Alex Campbell splashed the story across the pages of the *Inverness Courier* newspaper. And what a story it was! Campbell told of an encounter experienced by an anonymous well-known businessman and his wife who lived near Inverness. They had apparently been driving along the north side of the loch when they saw, to their amazement, a huge splashing in the water. They watched in complete shock as a massive animal, with a body not unlike that of a whale, broke the water. Campbell upped the intrigue and sensational nature of the story when he added that the water churned as the terrible thing surfaced, provoking cold fear in the pair.

There were, inevitably, those who were skeptical of the encounter. And particularly so when the identities of the mystery man and his wife were revealed: they were John Mackay and his wife, who just happened to be the owners of a hotel at Drumnadrochit. The press, and particularly the *New York Herald Tribune*, were openly suspicious of the story and inferred that, just perhaps, the Mackays had concocted the tale to ensure that flocks of tourists descended on the loch—and on the hotel, of course. It was a theory vehemently denied by the Mackays. Had the case been a solitary one, the media might have had a valid point. But the reports kept flooding in. That denizen of the deep, as Alex Campbell so famously labeled it, was here to stay.

The Loch Ness alligator?

Nine days after the Mackay story was publicized, the beastie was seen again. This time, those lucky enough to see the animal were Alexander Shaw and his son. At Whitefield House, which offers a splendid panoramic view of the loch from a height of more than one hundred feet, the pair saw a large wake develop, followed by an impressively sized back breaking the surface. The MacLennan family, residents of Temple Pier, also encountered strange animals in Loch Ness in 1933—and on more than one occasion, too. They were adamant that the long-necked beast sported flippers and was around thirty feet in length. A pair of large humps was seen in Loch Ness on May 27 by Nora Thompson, who stood transfixed, watching the animal until it quickly sunk beneath the waves amid a huge, almighty splash.

Maybe strangest of all the stories was that which the media highlighted on June 7. It was the sighting by none other than a pilot who, while flying over the loch near Urquhart Castle, saw below him something that was distinctly alligator-like in appearance and which was around twenty-five feet long and four feet wide. It's interesting that the word "alligator" was used, as Miss K. MacDonald had described seeing a crocodile-like animal in the River Ness one year earlier—albeit an animal of a much smaller size to that seen by the pilot.

The world was amazed by the events of the early summer of 1933. And the press could not get enough of it. To everyone's delight, the beastly best was yet to come.

Terror on the road

There's no doubt that in terms of Nessie lore, July 22, 1933, was both history-making and groundbreaking. That was the date on which Mr. and Mrs. George Spicer had an encounter with a large and lumbering beast at Loch Ness. Clearly, as Mr. Spicer's words demonstrated, they wished this had never occurred. Most people would likely love to see one of the Nessies, but not the Spicers; it was a traumatic and terrifying event that they tried their very best to forget. Unfortunately for them, they failed.

George Spicer was a man with a busy job: he was a director of a well-respected tailors in London called Messrs. Todhouse, Reynard and Co. So when the opportunity came up for a vacation, he and his wife jumped at it. They chose to take a trip to Scotland for a bit of tranquility and relaxation. What a mistake that turned out to be! It was around 4:00 p.m. on the Spicers' final day in Scotland when their holiday turned into a veritable nightmare. As the pair drove along the road that links Foyers and Dores, in a southerly direction, Mrs. Spicer suddenly screamed. And she had a very good reason to scream. Somewhere in the region of 600 feet in front of them, a bizarre-looking animal loomed out of the bushes that dominated the roadside. At first, all that could be seen was what looked like a large trunk. As they got closer, however, the situation quickly changed.

George Spicer described the animal as being hideous, an absolute affront against nature. What particularly struck him—and what provoked his comments—was the way the thing moved. It did not do so like any normal animal. Rather, it lumbered across the road in a series of odd jerks and coils; something which, for Spicer and his wife, was reminiscent of a massive worm. He said that by the time the shocked pair reached the section of the road where the monster had appeared, it was already gone. Nevertheless, evidence of its presence was still there: the surrounding bracken had clearly been flattened by something large and heavy.

Of several other things the Spicers were sure: the beast was at least five feet in height and could easily have inflicted severe damage on their car. Its skin was a gray color, not unlike the dark gray skin of an elephant. Oddly, Spicer also said that the monster seemed to be carrying something on its back. He admitted that both he and his wife remained traumatized by the awful sight for weeks.

Although skeptics suggest that the Spicers saw nothing stranger than a line of otters or deer, for the monster-hunting community, the case remains a classic. It must be said that the story has been expanded over the years—not by the Spicers, it should be stressed. The issue of the beast carrying something on its back has led to controversial assertions that the "something" was the body of a lamb. True or not, it's intriguing to think that the monsters, on rare occasions, may take to the land to secure a tasty meal, or several.

A near-collision with a creature of the deep

Six months later, a Nessie was once *again* seen on land. On this occasion, the witness was a man named Arthur Grant, of Glen Urquhart. That Grant was a student veterinarian added to the weight and credibility of his report. A keen motorcyclist, the twenty-one-year-old was on the roads, heading home at around 1:00 a.m., when he very nearly became the first person to ever have a head-on collision with a Nessie! Fortunately, however, neither monster nor motorcyclist were injured.

The night sky was dominated by a powerful, eerie moon, which meant that Grant had a very good view of the beast as it loomed before him, caught in the glare of his motorbike's headlight. It was at a distance of around 120 feet that Grant first caught sight of something unusual. Exactly how unusual it was became apparent nearly immediately. Grant said of his sighting that he was practically on top of the monster when its tiny head—set atop an elongated neck—suddenly turned in his direction. Evidently just as shocked as Grant was, the monster made two bounds across the road, headed down to the loch, and vanished into its depths with an almighty splash. Grant brought his motorbike to what was literally a screeching halt and, demonstrating his spirited character, gave chase! It was quickly clear to him, however, that as indicated by the huge splash, the monster had made good its escape. Nevertheless, in the time between first seeing it and when it fled for the dark waters, Grant was able to get an excellent view of his quarry. He described the monster as having a bulky body, flippers rather than legs, and a thick, approximately six-foot-long tail that looked like it could inflict significant damage. As for its overall size, Grant suggested somewhere close to twenty feet.

Skeptics claim that Grant fabricated the story; however, it should be noted that he was insistent he saw a monster and even made a statement to that effect to the Edinburgh-based Veterinary Society. Given that he was a student veterinarian, it seems unlikely that he would have taken the risk of recklessly lying to the Veterinary Society. A prank on the press is one thing; risking one's entire future career would have been quite another entirely. Grant's statement to the Society is an important one, as it adds some intriguing data to his original report.

As he pointed out, he knew more than a bit about the world of natural history, given his profession. As a result, he had pondered deeply on the nature of the monster. Interestingly, he said that the beast seemed to be a chimera—that is to say, a combination of several creatures. The head of the monster, he explained, was eel-like. Or it could have been snake-like; he wasn't altogether sure.

The body resembled that of a plesiosaur. The eyes were large—although, admittedly, he had only seen one. Logic dictates, however, that both eyes would have been uniform in nature and appearance. The skin of the animal, he reported, was like that of a whale.

The plesiosaur: a flawed candidate

It was accounts like those of Arthur Grant and the Spicers that quickly led to the development of the theory that the Loch Ness Monsters represent nothing less than a relic population of plesiosaurs. There's no doubt that this is the most popular and engaging theory for the Nessies, and one which the Scottish tourist industry, Hollywood, and the media love to promote whenever possible. Unfortunately for those willing to put their money on this admittedly attractive theory, the bad news is that the chance of the Nessies being plesiosaurs is slim to the point of being almost impossible.

First, there is the not-insignificant fact that the plesiosaur surfaced around 250 million years ago and died out around 66-65 million years ago. As the fossil record has conclusively shown, Plesiosaurs lived in saltwater environments—our planet's oceans. Loch Ness, meanwhile, is a freshwater loch. Yes, there is evidence of the occasional plesiosaur in a freshwater environment, but the bulk of the cases are not suggestive of entire colonies of the beasts inhabiting freshwater bodies. It's far more likely and plausible that they wandered into them and died there. And, yes, there exist both a freshwater crocodile and a saltwater crocodile. But the comparison is meaningless without evidence that plesiosaurs were 100 percent comfortable in both freshwater and saltwater.

And more on the matter of extinction vs. non-extinction: let's take note of the fact that—as the fossil-record shows—there is not a single bit of evidence to suggest that plesiosaurs (anywhere on the planet) survived beyond 60-plus million years ago. Yes, we have fossilized examples of plesiosaurs. But, no, they don't date from—for example and hypothetically—20 million years ago, or even 5 or 1 million years ago. They all date from the precise period in which science tells us they came to an end.

And even if plesiosaurs *did* survive—against just about all the odds conceivable—into the modern era, they could not have made their way into Loch Ness until around the end of the last Ice Age, for one simple reason: Loch Ness didn't exist until then. Up until that time, the area (the Great Glen) was—for all intents and purposes—a vast block of ice. So if they didn't enter the Loch until approximately 10,000 years ago, up until that point they must have lived in the ocean waters. But then there's the problem of why we haven't found any ocean-based remains of plesiosaurs dating back 13,000 or 20,000 years, for example.

If evidence *had* been found of plesiosaurs off the coast of Scotland, and just before the end of the last Ice Age, each and every one of us should be even a bit impressed. But nope, the evidence is always tens of millions of years old. If the plesiosaur survived beyond 65 million years ago, why is the evidence to support such a scenario 100 percent absent? Because there is no evidence, that's why.

And now we come to the final observation on this monster matter. Plesiosaurs, despite what some might assume, were not fish. They were reptiles. That means they had to surface to take in oxygen. Crocodiles—which, of course, are also reptiles—can remain underwater for up to around two hours at a time. So, keeping that in mind, how about a bit of hypothesizing?

The problem of the lack of sightings

If the Nessies *are* plesiosaurs, then let's say that at any given time there are around twenty of them in the loch, ranging from (a) young and small to (b) large and old. That would be a reasonable figure to ensure the continuation of a healthy herd. Let's also say they, like crocodiles, can stay submerged, without taking in oxygen, for up to two hours at a time. This means that in any one day, each plesiosaur would have to surface around twelve times. Twenty plesiosaurs, surfacing twelve times a day (at a minimum, I should stress), would equate to 240 surfacing events in every single twenty-four-hour period. Multiply that by a week and the figure is elevated to 1,680. Then multiply that by fifty-two weeks in a year and the figure becomes a massive 87,360 annually.

Even if 90 percent of the surfacing events went unnoticed or unreported (for fear of ridicule, perhaps), that would still mean in excess of *8,000 reports per year, every year.* But the fact is that the number of sightings reported per annum equates to barely a handful. And let's say there are only around ten plesiosaurs at any particular time in the loch (rather than my suggested twenty); well, that still means a potential 43,680 cases of the animals surfacing across 365 days. Finally, there is the matter of Nessie's famous long neck. A study of fossilized remains of plesiosaurs has demonstrated that the animals simply were not built to raise their necks high out of the water in the proud and prominent fashion that has been attributed to the Loch Ness Monsters.

Clearly, there is something very wrong here. And what is wrong is the reliance on the plesiosaur theory, which is without doubt woefully inadequate when it comes to trying to explain what lurks deep in Loch Ness. If only this inadequate theory could become as extinct as the plesiosaur itself. Yet it has endured since

1933 without a single shred of evidence to support it. Ironically, a fascinating piece of evidence—a photograph—turned up in 1933 that adds further weight to the argument that the monsters are not plesiosaurs. Read on.

9

Muddying the Waters

Sunday, November 12, 1933, was the date on which the most curious and controversial photograph of all was taken of an alleged Nessie. It remains controversial more than eighty years later—not because it's of a too-good-to-be-true nature, but as a result of the fact that the creature is so weird-looking. Indeed, its appearance is at extreme odds with what so many other eyewitnesses claim to have encountered at the loch.

The witness that day was one Hugh Gray, an employee of the British Aluminum Company. The hot and sunny location of the sighting was near where the mouth of the River Foyers and Loch Ness come together, and the time was around noon. It can be said that Gray was the perfect person to see the creature, as the company he worked for had its premises within walking distance of the place where the encounter occurred—a nearly sheer bluff with a height of about fifty feet, overlooking the loch and dominated by dense woods.

According to Gray, after attending a Sunday morning mass, he went for a walk, as he did every Sunday. It was a bright and sunny day, he said, and the loch was glistening. Suddenly, something broke the surface of Loch Ness. And it was of large proportions. Very large proportions. As luck would have it, Gray had a camera with him and managed to get a shot of the animal as it not just surfaced but seemed to float almost completely on top of the water. An utterly amazed Gray stood staring at the odd spectacle until the animal submerged, amid a thrashing of its tail.

A photographic enigma

Hugh Gray's picture is, admittedly, an odd one. As a result, it has been interpreted in varying ways—sometimes *wildly* interpreted. For the skeptics, the most obvious popular answer is that the photo is an innocent, unintended double-exposure of a portion of the loch and a Labrador dog swimming directly towards the camera, holding a stick in its mouth, and with its black nose and muzzle on show. It's a theory that has been endorsed by the mainstream media—unfortunately without any real, meaningful, critical analysis. There are, however, very good reasons why it can be said that the photo clearly is *not* a double exposure and does not show a faithful hound returning a stick to its master.

Yes, one can see what looks like the face of a dog facing the camera—if one chooses to do so. This is, however, undeniably a case of nothing more than pareidolia, a recognized phenomenon that occurs when the human eye attempts to interpret random imagery in the context of something familiar and recognizable. Examples might include seeing faces in clouds, or the visage of Elvis in a peanut-butter-and-jelly sandwich. The Gray photo, however, is not one which has pareidolia and a swimming, playing dog at its heart. What it does have at its heart is a creature that is clearly large, curiously floating atop the water, and lacking the long neck that so many witnesses have reported. It is, you may surmise, the oddly missing extended neck that has provoked so much controversy. But if Hugh Gray's photo doesn't show a dog, then what does it show? Let's take a look.

The Loch Ness Monster surfaces and shows its face

Analyzing the image

To the left of the photo is an oddly positioned but thick-looking tail. That there is a degree of haziness present in the photo suggests the tail may have been thrashing violently at the time the picture was taken (which Gray suggested); something which caused water to spray into the air and make the image appear slightly out of focus and misty. Plus, it is slightly overexposed, which only adds to the limited clarity issues. Nevertheless, we also see a fairly thick body that clearly shows a pair of small appendages on what would be the creature's right side. The obvious and logical presumption is that two identical appendages are on the left side too, although admittedly we cannot be 100 percent sure of that since the photo only shows one view of the animal.

The most important part of the photo is the extreme right-hand side. There is very little doubt that what is captured on celluloid, and for all to see, is the face of a Nessie. It very much resembles the head of a turtle, and has a distinct beak-like appearance. One can even make out what looks like a small eye and an open mouth that seems to show evidence of a tongue. Possibly most important of all, the shadow of the head can clearly be seen below it, and reflecting off the rippling waters of the loch. Then there is the matter of how high the animal is. It's practically completely *out* of the water.

Loch Ness Monster authority Roland Watson has noticed and commented on this curious aspect of the Gray photo. He has suggested the monsters of Loch Ness may possess a form of inbuilt internal buoyancy—something which would allow them to float on the surface in the very odd fashion described by Gray.

Ted Holiday was a dedicated seeker of Nessie who started out believing the Nessies are flesh-and-blood animals but who, in the early 1970s, radically changed his views—as we shall see later. Before his mind swung over to the dark and supernatural side, Holiday was a champion of the theory that Hugh Gray had filmed a living, breathing creature of unknown origins and identity. He also concluded that the monster captured by Gray was somewhere between twenty and thirty feet in length.

Roy Mackal, also fascinated by the Loch Ness Monster, commented on a particular theory that has relevance to one specific aspect of Hugh Gray's photo: the turtle-like head. He noted, correctly, that the Leatherback Turtle can grow to impressive sizes and weights: up to ten feet in length and to weights of over a ton. Problematic, however, is the fact that Leatherback Turtles do not have long tails. And, like all turtles, they give birth on land. This latter issue effectively rules out turtles as being the guilty parties, since by now at least one of the millions of people who have visited Loch Ness would surely have stumbled on at least one sizable egg of such an immense beast.

Super-sized salamanders in Scotland

A far more thought-provoking theory has been suggested by Steve Plambeck. He suspects the Nessies may be giant salamanders and has diligently studied the Gray photo. The salamander theory actually dates back to the earliest years of Nessie lore, but certainly no one has dug quite so deeply and dedicatedly as Plambeck. Salamanders are amphibians that are noted for their long tails, blunt heads, and short limbs, and which—in the case of the Chinese giant salamander—can reach lengths of six feet. Is it possible that some salamanders could grow much larger, even to the extent of fifteen to twenty-five feet? Incredible? Yes. Implausible? Maybe not.

Steve Plambeck says that the Nessies are likely to be creatures that derive their oxygen from the water. Add to that the distinct lack of large numbers of sightings, and what we have, Plambeck believes, is some form of creature that spends the bulk of its time on the bed of the loch. Or at least very near to it. Only on occasion do the animals venture to the higher levels, something which would account for the occasional encounters and images caught on sonar. Plambeck also suggests that when the monsters do take to the higher levels of Loch Ness, they do so along its sides— which are the main areas where Loch Ness's fish populations dwell. In other words, the monsters surface chiefly when they are feeding. Plambeck notes, "Such behavior is only consistent with a fish, or aquatic amphibian, which can extract all of its needed oxygen directly from the water."

In that sense, Plambeck makes a persuasive argument when it comes to the matter of the creatures of Loch Ness possibly being huge salamanders, or at the very least another kind of large, unknown amphibian. It's a theory also noted by researcher "Erika."

She says of such a scenario that China's giant salamander is a creature hardly noted for its speed or its time spent out of the water. Indeed, as she correctly states, the creature spends much of its life at the bottom of large bodies of water, where it lies in wait of passing fish that are destined to become tasty meals. She makes the point that taking into consideration the fact that the Chinese giant salamander is a bottom-dweller, and one that is rarely seen, it's not impossible that a similar creature in Loch Ness could remain largely unnoticed.

Loch Ness Monster authority Roland Watson has also waded into this controversy, admitting that "I am a bit partial to a fish-like amphibian or amphibian-like fish theory myself."

Shifting shapes in the 1930s

The big problem with the salamander scenario is the matter of the long neck. Or, in relation to the salamander, the distinct and glaring *lack* of a long neck. One suggestion, not entirely implausible, is that the presumed coiling neck that so many have reported is actually the tail of the salamander, albeit misinterpreted by the witnesses— and possibly as a direct result of cultural conditioning and pop-culture imagery of what the Nessies are *supposed* to look like. There is, however, another theory, one which goes right back to some of the earliest reports of the monsters of Loch Ness. It's the theory that the Nessies of the 1930s were supernatural shapeshifters, one and all, just like their counterparts of centuries earlier.

Let's look at the facts as we know them. In 1880, Duncan Mac-Donald had a terrifying eye-to-eye encounter with something that resembled a giant, goat-sized frog. There was the matter of that tusked beast seen in the waters of the River Ness, in 1932, by Miss K. MacDonald. Lieutenant McP Fordyce described seeing an animal that walked like an elephant, that looked like a combination of a "very large horse and a camel," and which was shaggy in appearance. Arthur Grant's sighting was of something more akin to a plesiosaur. Mr. and Mrs. George Spicer encountered a creature that had a jerky, wormy gait and which provoked both nightmares and what practically sounds like post-traumatic stress disorder.

And, as we have just seen, Hugh Gray photographed an animal with a beak-like, turtle-style head. It had absolutely no neck of any significance whatsoever, and its stubby appendages were clearly not sizable plesiosaur-like flippers of the type Arthur Grant was sure he saw. Nor were they anything that might have allowed the creature to walk on land like an elephant.

It must be noted that in the early 1930s, a period in which technology was developing in leaps and bounds, the mysterious tales of body-morphing water-horses and kelpies held nowhere near the sway they did in centuries previously. Times were changing. But the day eventually came—as we shall see later—when those old terrors and superstitions surrounding all things of a kelpie nature eventually resurfaced and took hold of fear-filled minds and souls. And something else resurfaced at Loch Ness in the 1930s. Or, rather, someone else: none other than Aleister Crowley.

10

Crowley and the Creature

When the story of the Loch Ness Monster kicked off in spectacular style in 1933, none other than our old friend Aleister Crowley was keen to embroil himself in the controversy; *very* keen, in fact. Of course, this was two decades after Crowley had exited Boleskine House, but that did not prevent him from leaving his own unique impression on the formative years of Nessie lore. In November 1933, the *Empire News* asked Crowley for his personal views on the Loch Ness Monster. The result of the invitation was that Crowley penned an entire article on the subject, published on November 12. Its title: "The Magician of Loch Ness: Uncanny Happenings at Manor of Boleskine."

Crowley told the readers that he was highly intrigued by the growing controversy surrounding the Loch Ness Monster, and particularly so the stories that described some kind of huge, large-eyed monster on the loose. He couldn't fail to note the fact that Loch Ness was brimming with high-strangeness; after all, he had experienced it personally at Boleskine House. He wrote, "long before I purchased the Manor it was already the place around which a score of legends had been woven. All of them of a mysterious nature. Thus the head of old Lord Lovat, who was beheaded after the '45 [the Jacobite Rebellion of 1745], was believed to roll up and down the corridors of the rambling old place. There was another legend that a lunatic had murdered his mother by smashing her brains out against the wall, and that she returned at times to pick them up again. These alone had sufficed to give Boleskine an evil reputation, and my own experiences there by no means diminished that evil reputation."

Ancient creatures at Boleskine House

Although Crowley played down any personal knowledge of the Loch Ness Monster, it seems to be highly likely he knew something—and maybe even a great deal—of what was going on within the black heart of those vast, expansive depths. It is, surely, no coincidence that when he lived at Boleskine House, Crowley had a large sign posted outside that read, *Beware the Ichthyosaurus!* Another practically screamed, *The Deinotheriums are out today!*

For those who may not know, the ichthyosaurus was of the ichthyosaur genus; marine reptiles that surfaced in the Triassic era and died out in the Jurassic period. They were creatures that began life on land, but then gravitated to the waters—rather than the other way around, which was the case for so many now-extinct animals tens of millions of years ago. They were very much dolphin-like and fish-like in appearance, and extended in length from barely one meter to roughly seventeen. How curious, then, that Crowley should have kept people away from his home with warnings of a beast that—like the Loch Ness Monsters—had associations with both the land and the water and could grow to notable sizes.

As for deinotherium, it is an ancient Greek term that translates to—wait for it—*terrible beast*. One could argue that this was a jokey reference to Crowley himself, since he became infamously known as "the Great Beast." On the other hand, consider this:

deinotherium was an animal of the Miocene period that was very much elephant-like in appearance. It's intriguing to note that, as we have seen, a number of witnesses to the monsters of the loch have described them as having elephant-like skin in both color and texture. Clearly, then, Crowley knew *far* more of the monster than many might suspect—even if, for his own obscure reasons, he chose not to publicly overemphasize that knowledge.

Crowley remained interested in the Loch Ness creatures right up until the time of his death on December 1, 1947. One more thing on Crowley: it's important to note that he came to believe he was the reincarnation of a man named Edward Kelly, a controversial figure who plunged himself into the dark world of magick in the sixteenth century. Why is that so important? Specifically because Edward Kelly plays a major role in the development of the weirder side of the saga of the Loch Ness Monster.

A spymaster, a magician, and a world of sorcery

Born Edward Talbot in 1555, Edward Kelly and his family originated in Uí Maine, Connacht, Ireland. As someone convicted of the crime of counterfeiting, Kelly had his ears violently sliced off as punishment. Although few would ever know this, since his hearing remained intact, he barely ever removed the black cap that was pulled down tight on his head, and he wore his hair long. He also had intriguing associations: he spent much of his time digging into the worlds of the occult and alchemy, along with a man named Dr. John Dee. Dee was a shadowy Machiavellian character, born in London in 1527, who played a major role in the early years of the British Secret Service created by "spymaster" Sir Francis Walsingham. Dee was a student of both astrology and magic and possessed one of England's largest libraries on the dark arts. He was a person one crossed at one's peril.

According to both Kelly and Dee, in 1582 they succeeded in doing nothing less than communicating with an angel named Uriel. One year later, Dee deciphered the so-called Enochian language—the hitherto secret language of the angels. Dee did so in tried and tested fashion: via gazing into a crystal ball while in a decidedly tripped-out state of mind. Not only that, but the pair also had encounters with what they called "little men" who flew around the skies in what was termed "a little fiery cloud." It doesn't take much to conclude that what Dee and Kelly were describing sounds very similar to what people say they witnessed in UFO encounters today: strange, small humanoids and a brightly lit craft of the flying saucer variety.

The paranormal pair spent a great deal of time touring Europe, exposing countless numbers of people to their work and findings, including Emperor Rudolf II, the king of Croatia, Bohemia, Germany, and Hungary. The king was highly impressed by Kelly's skills, to the extent that he knighted him on February 23, 1590. Bad times were looming on the horizon, however. Very bad. In May 1591, Kelly was imprisoned for killing a man—Jiri Hunkler—in a duel. He was released, however, when he told Emperor Rudolf that he was close to perfecting the art of transmuting base metals into gold; the ultimate goal of the alchemist.

Yet when Kelly failed to deliver on his promise, he was once again slung in jail. While trying to escape, he fell from the jail's outer wall and broke his leg, something which ultimately led to his death. As for Dee, he returned to England only to find his home in ruins and his precious library utterly plundered. His priceless, cherished old books were gone forever. Dee lived out his last years in squalor and poverty in Mortlake, London, dying at the age of eighty-two in 1608.

In curious and unsettling fashion, the pair—tied in strange fashion to Aleister Crowley—would resurface centuries later in the affair of the Loch Ness Monster, as we shall see. Before we get to that, however, there's the matter of an audacious hoax.

— 11 —

Hoaxing the Horror of Loch Ness

There can be absolutely no doubt that of all the many and varied photographs that have been taken which purport to show a mysterious creature in the waters of Loch Ness, the one that provokes controversy on an unparalleled scale is known, somewhat incorrectly, as the "Surgeon's Photograph." It was taken one year after Nessie hysteria began. I say "somewhat incorrectly" because the surgeon in question actually took two photos, although just one of the pair has become famous. The other languishes in relative obscurity even to this day. For decades the famous photo was championed by Nessie seekers as hard evidence that Loch Ness harbors monsters. Today, however, its reputation is in tatters.

The story dates back to April 19, 1934, which was when one Colonel Robert Kenneth Wilson claimed to have both seen and photographed one of the Nessies. The story seemed solid, since Wilson was a respected London-based gynecologist; hardly the sort of person to perpetrate a hoax, right? Wrong. It was a story—and photo, of course—that the *Daily Mail* newspaper was more than happy to share with its readers; although at the time, Wilson flatly refused to have his name attached to the story, preferring instead to just focus on how he came to be in the right place at the right moment.

The controversy of cropping

There's no denying the photo was taken in Loch Ness, and there's no doubt that it shows what appears to be a prominent head and neck above the surface of the water. But here's the problem: the famous—arguably iconic—photo that was presented by the *Daily Mail*, and which can be found in the pages of numerous books and periodicals and on countless blogs and websites, is actually a carefully cropped version of the original. It was deliberately cropped in a close-up fashion to make the neck look impressively large. When one looks at the original panoramic image, however, and compares both the head and neck to the size of the surrounding ripples on the loch, it's easy to see that the monster is not just small but ridiculously small.

Hoaxing Scotland's most famous monster

Revealing the ruse

It was in 1994 that the complicated and convoluted truth was finally made public. The monster was actually a sculptured head, one that was affixed to a toy submarine! It all began with a man named Marmaduke Wetherell. He was a big-game hunter of the extremely pathetic type who think it's cool and macho to slaughter elephants, giraffes, or Cecil the lion. In December 1933, nearly a half year prior to the publication of the Surgeon's Photograph, the *Daily Mail* pretty much assassinated Wetherell's character after he loudly stated that he had found footprints of a monster at Loch Ness. But they weren't; Wetherell was the victim of a hoax. The prints were those of a hippopotamus, most likely formed by an umbrella stand made out of a hippo foot. Wetherell was both enraged and embarrassed and decided to get his revenge on the *Daily Mail*.

The conspirators go to work

Wetherell's son-in-law was one Christian Spurling, who was a sculptor. Spurling—using plastic-wood materials purchased by Wetherell's son, Ian—created a Nessie-like head and neck, which was then carefully attached to a toy submarine. Also in on the act was an insurance agent named Maurice Chambers. The game, as Sherlock Holmes was so fond of saying, was afoot. A test run, in a small pond, was successful. And so it was soon time for the conspirators to perform the final act. The particular stretch of water where the famous photos were taken was, by all accounts, somewhere near the Altsaigh Tea House.

With the submarine carefully placed in the water, and with the neck and head standing proud and tall, the photos were quickly taken, after which the monster was scuttled and disappeared beneath the water—never to be seen again. It was then Chambers's role to provide the less-than-priceless pictures to his friend Colonel Robert Kenneth Wilson, who became the fall guy in the saga by selling the famous picture to the *Daily Mail*. The photo remained a matter of controversy until 1994, when then ninety-year-old Christian Spurling finally fessed up. Five years later, a book titled *Nessie: The*

Surgeon's Photograph Exposed, written by David M. Martin and Alastair Boyd, was published and the entire sorry tale exploded.

It's important to note, however, that this unfortunate state of affairs did not prevent credible sightings from continuing to be reported.

12

From the '40s to the '50s

It should come as no surprise to learn that the number of sightings of Loch Ness Monsters dropped off dramatically in the late 1930s and remained at very low levels throughout much of the 1940s. There was a very good reason for this. People were far less concerned about what was going on in a Scottish loch and far more concerned about a certain Austrian maniac who, in 1934, came to power in Germany. His name, or course, was Adolf Hitler.

When, in 1939, the governments of both Britain and France declared war on Nazi Germany—after its September 1939 invasion of Poland—it marked the beginning of six turbulent and carnage-filled years. Survival, not Nessie-seeking, was the main thing on most people's minds. Nevertheless, there were a few notable Nessie encounters reported during the time when Hitler tried—but thankfully failed—to conquer Europe and then the rest of the planet.

The monster during warfare

August 18, 1941, was the date of a particularly notable encounter with one of the monsters of the loch, given that it was seen by no less than dozens of people. The specific location was the waters off of Glendoe Pier, where a creature, with a long neck and a humped body of around eighteen feet long, was encountered. Reportedly the animal was seen for in excess of ten minutes as it raced around the water at a surprisingly fast pace.

Then there was the wartime report of one C. B. Farrell, who was attached to the military's Royal Observer Corps during the hostilities. His job was to scan the skies for incoming German fighter planes and bombers. Given his position with the ROC, Farrell was fortunate enough to have with him at the time of his sighting—which was roughly around 5:00 a.m.—a pair of binoculars. They provided him with an amazing sight: a large animal with an approximately four-foot-long finned neck. According to Farrell, the creature repeatedly ducked its head into the water, then raised it out, shaking it wildly. It was Farrell's opinion that the animal was possibly feeding on shoals of fish.

The summer of 1946 was when the Atkinson family saw a monster in the waters off Dores. It was purely down to chance that they got to see the beast: as they drove past the loch, their car suffered a flat tire. Mr. Atkinson quickly pulled over to the side of the road and proceeded to change the tire—only to be interrupted by the sight of a large, long-necked, gray-colored creature. The beast's presence evidently had a traumatic effect on Mrs. Atkinson, who experienced chills and fears relative to *what else* of a terrifying nature might be in the loch—never mind just the Nessies! Christmas 1948 was approaching when Mrs. Russell Ellice and her two children encountered a long-necked Nessie in the waters near Brachla. Unlike the aforementioned Mrs. Atkinson, the Ellice family was delighted to see the mysterious creature. Indeed, it made Mrs. Ellice's day.

A new decade dawns

While the 1950s offered Nessie seekers new and credible cases, the decade also offered a couple of controversial photographs that still, to this very day, provoke debate and raised voices in those domains where monster hunters hang out. In July 1951, a spectacular and controversy-filled photograph appeared in the pages of the UK's popular *Sunday Express* newspaper. No surprises concerning the subject matter. The photo in question was taken by a man named Lachlan Stuart, early on the morning of July 15. It showed what appeared to be three large, dark humps protruding prominently out of the waters of Loch Ness. The story, just like Nessie, surfaced quickly. Indeed, the newspaper ran the story and the attendant photo only one day after the encounter occurred. Even in the postwar period, Nessie was causing a stir and selling newspapers.

It could be argued that Stuart was the perfect person to see the monster, as he and his family owned land approximately one hundred feet above the loch, at Whitefield, pretty much directly opposite Urquhart Castle. It was fortunate—or suspicious—that Stuart had a box-camera with him at the time, which allowed him to get a clear picture of the beast and its prominent humps. Also present was a man named Taylor Hay, who claimed to have seen the creature, too.

Stuart's best guesstimate was that the humps were around five feet in length and between two and four feet in height. Interestingly, Stuart claimed to have seen some sort of commotion going on under the surface of the waves, too, and for a distance of around twenty feet. This led him to suspect a huge tail was wildly thrashing below, and which, therefore, suggested the presence of an animal of close to fifty feet in length. Stuart also said the beast had a sheep-like head; unfortunately, however, the head and neck submerged before Stuart was able to get his shot of that.

At one point, both men said, the animal came perilously close to the shore—which led them to back away to the safety of the surrounding trees—but then it retreated to a point around nine hundred feet out and sank below, never to resurface. It was, then, quite an experience. Or was it?

Not the real Nessie?

Richard Frere was someone with a deep interest in the stories of the Loch Ness Monster. He was, however, also deeply skeptical of the tales. That didn't stop him from investigating those same tales. In fact, he did so with gusto. In 1980, Frere visited the then newly opened Official Loch Ness Monster Expedition, where he spoke with Tony Harmsworth, a noted seeker of Nessie who had his own encounter with something strange in Loch Ness in 1986. According to Harmsworth, Frere, who died in 1999, personally saw Lachlan Stuart creating his bogus image of a Nessie. It was, so Frere maintained, an image that showed nothing stranger than three bales of hay covered by tarpaulins.

There are other problems, too: Lachlan Stuart claimed the photo was taken during the early morning hours. A study of the lighting of the photo, however, suggests it was taken during the evening. The most glaringly problematic issue, however, is the collective shape of the three humps. Most witnesses to the Nessies describe the humps as being smooth and elongated. In the Stuart photos, the humps are almost triangular in appearance. Indeed, looking at them, they almost resemble a trio of mini-pyramids floating on the waves of the loch. That this description and appearance is almost unique in Nessie history suggests that although the debate over the Lachlan Stuart photo continues, we should tread carefully on the matter of what it shows versus what it *alleges* to show.

Three years after the photo's publication, in December 1954, the crew of the Rival III fishing vessel had a curious encounter on Loch Ness. None of them caught sight of a Nessie—at least not visually. What they did do, however, was track on their sonar equipment a large, unknown object that shadowed the boat for a distance of around 2,500 feet, and at a depth of approximately 480 feet. Precisely what it was, was never determined.

The biggest Nessie of all

Peter A. Macnab's July 1955 photograph, of what appears to be the humped backs of a pair of Nessies—one large and the other significantly smaller—has been reproduced in numerous books and praised in glowing terms by the Nessie faithful. It's easy to understand why: the photo does, admittedly, look impressive. With Urquhart Castle to the right of the frame and the two Nessies to the left, the photo appears to be prime evidence of not just significantly sized monsters in Loch Ness, but ones that have the ability to reach *enormous* sizes. MacNab's legendary image suggests—based on the size of the castle—that the larger animal is close to *sixty feet* in length. But the photograph is not without its problems. And, when and where there's a problem, that usually smacks of a hoax.

Although the picture was taken in 1955, it was not publicized until 1957, in the pages of Constance Whyte's book *More Than a Legend*. When the image was revealed for all to see, it provoked amazement—as does the real Nessie when it surfaces. The problem with MacNab's photo is not what it shows or that it exists; the problem is that there are two versions of it. The late Roy Mackal —a dedicated seeker of Nessie—obtained a negative of the photo from MacNab and instantly noticed something odd. The photo that MacNab provided to Constance Whyte was not made from the negative given to Mackal. In both images, Urquhart Castle and a nearby clump of trees are reflected in the water. Problematic is the fact that the reflections are at variance with each other.

Two photos and a pair of cameras

MacNab, a respected bank manager, claimed that he took two separate photos with two different cameras. Fair enough. But that still doesn't explain one critical factor: MacNab also asserted that as he watched the beasts, they were continually on the move. Yet the two photos—despite the differences in the reflections, to angles of around four degrees, and the apparent use of two different cameras—show the alleged Nessies in exactly the same place in both photos. And I do mean *exactly*. On top of that, the Whyte photo shows a tree in the foreground, which is missing in the negative acquired by Mackal. Due to the angle at which both photos were taken, the tree should be present in both. Or should it?

Roland Watson has carefully studied the issue of the tree that is seemingly there one second and gone the next. He says that what has been perceived as a red flag may not be a red flag after all. He explains that the copy in the hands of Roy Mackal was "a zoom-in which was sufficient to exclude the foreground tree. The tree had not been edited out by nefarious means, but rather was just out of view in the new version."

For some people, Peter Macnab's picture is just too good to be true. For others, the possible anomalies suggest it's not good enough. For many, the image baffles as much as it intrigues. Reluctantly, it has to go in our "gray" basket until, or unless, something hitherto unknown one day appears that lays the matter to rest—one way or the other.

Most definitely not in our gray basket, however, is an amazing encounter that occurred as the 1950s gave way to a new decade.

13
The Dinsdale Affair

As a new era dawned, Loch Ness's reputation as a place of infinite strangeness and malignancy reached new levels. It was in 1960 that the then-owner of Boleskine House—a retired British Army Major named Edward Grant—shot himself in the very bedroom in which Aleister Crowley engaged in occult rites, wild orgies, and supernatural summoning. Grant's housekeeper, Anna MacLaren, was the unfortunate soul who stumbled upon the body of the major—after she had a sudden and curious premonition that he was not long for this world. When she ran to the room after hearing a single, loud shot while gardening at the back of the house, she was to be confronted by a nightmarish scene.

Upon reaching the house, MacLaren could see standing by the door the Major's little dog, Pickiwig. He was playing with a small piece of bone. For reasons we'll likely never know, given that the gunshot should have been her first priority, she asked him where he got it. Pickiwig's only reply was a friendly wag of his tail. MacLaren grabbed the bone and then headed to the bedroom. The sight before her was shocking in the extreme. Edward Grant was sitting in front of a large mirror, his head almost completely blown off his shoulders. Blood was splattered everywhere. Although in a state of hysteria, MacLaren had the presence of mind to call the police before fleeing the house. It turned out that Pickiwig's little treat was actually a portion of the major's skull and brain matter—Pickiwig almost certainly having been in the bedroom when the major took his life. Major Edward Grant's distraught wife, Mary, was left to pick up the pieces. Maybe even literally.

In a curious fashion, this is not the only occasion upon which suicide and Boleskine House have gone together, hand in glove. Only a few years before Grant's suicide, the house was owned by a famous British actor, George Sanders. His attempts to establish a pig farm on the grounds of the house failed miserably, and his partner—a Scottish Member of Parliament named Dennis Lorraine—was jailed on fraud charges. Sanders died of a self-induced drug overdose in April 1972, just after completing his final movie, a supernatural tale of the dead returning to life called *Psychomania*. It's a movie we will return to in due course, as it has a notable connection to the mystery of the Loch Ness creatures.

"I knew at once I was looking at the extraordinary humped back of some huge living creature"

The year 1960 was also when one of the most famous and controversial pieces of film footage of an alleged Loch Ness Monster was taken. It was the early morning of Saturday, April 23, and acclaimed Nessie-seeker Tim Dinsdale was several days into an expedition at the loch when something remarkable and—for Dinsdale—life-changing occurred. It was the final day of his trip, so it was a case of now or never. Very fortuitously for the man, it turned out to be *now*.

At roughly 8:30 a.m., Dinsdale, who had risen early, decided that as nothing unusual or amazing had happened in the previous five days, he might as well cut short his last day. So he bid both the loch and the monster farewell and headed off to his hotel. It was while driving through Upper Foyers—and still in the direction of his hotel—that Dinsdale saw something amazing. It was something dark, something that was moving across the surface of the loch at a distance he calculated was around 4,000 feet. Given the circumstances, Dinsdale remained surprisingly calm and collected.

Indeed, he did his best not to get overexcited: he brought the car to a halt, turned off the engine, and reached for his binoculars. Whatever the thing was, Dinsdale could see that it was of appreciable size. It was of a mahogany color and somewhat egg-shaped. On its left side was a dark patch—of what, Dinsdale had no idea. Interestingly, his instant thought was that the contour and color reminded him of an African buffalo, with plenty of girth and standing noticeably out of the water. As the creature suddenly began to move, Dinsdale could see ripples developing in the water, and, in his own immortal words in *Loch Ness Monster*, "I knew at once I was looking at the extraordinary humped back of some huge living creature."

Dinsdale's calmness was now utterly gone: he raced to grab and turn on his 16mm Bolex cine-camera—which had a 135mm telephoto lens and was already perched on its tripod in the car. In seconds, Dinsdale was filming the mysterious blob. He later said that, as he watched, he couldn't fail to notice that the thing left a definite V-shaped wake in the water and appeared to be slowly— as in *very* slowly—submerging. That's when things turned from exciting to stressful. Dinsdale was extremely low on film, and he realized that if he kept filming from his then-current position, he might use up all the footage without capturing a clearer, close-up shot of the assumed animal. So Dinsdale took a sudden decision. He stopped filming, jumped into his car, and shot away at high speed, careering along the road to Lower Foyers, then across a field, and finally down to the water's edge. Disastrously, the creature was no longer in sight. Mind you, he still had approximately four minutes of film of the subject.

The footage goes public and the military gets involved

Despite Dinsdale's determination to keep the affair, and the footage, secret, word soon got out within the monster-hunting community. It wasn't at all long before the British media was hot on the trail of the monster, of Dinsdale, and of his potentially priceless film. On June 13, 1960, the *Daily Mail* newspaper ran Dinsdale's story, along with four stills from the footage. He also appeared on the BBC's popular current-affairs show, *Panorama*. Dinsdale and his monster film were big news. He was deluged with mail, phone calls, and personal visits—not just from the media but from the public, too. It was a wild and crazy time for the monster hunter; a time that ensured his pursuit of Nessie was destined to go from strength to strength.

There was a major development in the story of Tim Dinsdale's forty feet of film in 1965. It was all thanks to a man named David James. As well as being a persistent pursuer of the Nessies, James was also a former member of the British Parliament. And as such, he had a lot of contacts and influence in the government, including access to personnel from what was called JARIC, the Joint Air Reconnaissance Center based at Royal Air Force Brampton, Huntingdon, England. JARIC's five hundred or so staff were experts at studying film footage—and, sometimes, hazy and hard-to-define footage, which was, and still is, certainly a good way to describe Dinsdale's film. Plus, studying film of an alleged Loch Ness Monster was a welcome break for the JARIC people, whose work was generally focused on analyzing footage of Russian fighter planes, bombers, and missile bases.

Not only did JARIC carefully scrutinize Dinsdale's footage, but they also came to a remarkable conclusion. According to JARIC files housed at the National Archives, Kew, England, the object was likely "not a surface vessel," such as a small boat. The team said that "one can presumably rule out the idea that it is any sort of submarine vessel for various reasons which leaves the conclusion that it is probably an animate object." Although critics such as Dr. Maurice Burton suggested the whole thing was a case of mistaken identity—of nothing more remarkable than a boat—the monster-hunting community was delighted. Roy P. Mackal said, "The JARIC analysis is important as an independent and expert study, free of either pro or con monster bias."

Loch Ness expert Peter Costello also noted something important in the Dinsdale film, namely that "the pattern of the wake and wash" around the supposed monster were "very different" from those of a boat that was seen and filmed by Dinsdale shortly afterwards.

And things don't end there. David James persuaded JARIC to look at yet more footage—specifically, footage secured by the Loch Ness Investigation Bureau (LNIB), an organization to which James belonged. The LNIB was dedicated to on-site investigations; at one point, it had more than one thousand members. Of the approximately thirty seconds of film the bureau supplied, taken of something in Loch Ness on October 18, 1962—something that was humped and clearly animate—JARIC concluded it did not show a wave, but a solid body that had a glistening appearance. Additional film, also taken in 1962, impressed JARIC, leading to their belief that the object was possibly a living creature. Then, in August 1965, a woman named Elizabeth Hall—also of the LNIB—filmed nine seconds of footage that showed two wakes on the water, moving parallel to each other. JARIC couldn't say what made the wakes, but its staff was pretty certain that the wakes were around nine feet away from each other—which effectively ruled out small boats, due to the danger of collision—and one was around seven and a half to eight feet in front of the other.

Together, these investigations contributed to a significant period in the decades-long search for Nessie. Yet the 1960s were also noted as the period in which the supernatural aspect of the Loch Ness Monster resurfaced, and the old days of the supernatural kelpies finally returned.

14

A Holiday at Loch Ness

In this vein, it's time now for me to demonstrate the sheer extent to which exposure to Loch Ness, and its attendant monsters and mysteries, can majorly affect a person's mindset and opinions regarding the nature of what's afoot in the dark waters. We only have to take a look at the strange and ultimately tragic saga of Frederick William Holiday—to his friends and colleagues, Ted Holiday—to see what I mean. It was hardly surprising that Holiday, a child of the 1920s, should have become enthused and excited by the explosion of interest in the Loch Ness Monster in 1933. He was, after all, a twelve-year-old boy at the time, one for whom adventures, unusual animals, and mysterious places were at the forefront of his young mind.

It was not until 1962, however, that Holiday, a skilled angler, was able to make the trip of a lifetime. He did so in an old van packed with all the essentials of a Nessie hunt, such as cameras, a sleeping bag, and even fishing rods—although one suspects a fishing rod would hardly have been a suitable tool for reeling in a huge, marauding leviathan of the deep, one quite possibly of supernatural and deadly proportions!

"Loch Ness is not a water by which to linger"

From the outset, Holiday was of the opinion that the Loch Ness Monsters were all too real. The question of exactly what they were, however, was an entirely different matter, and something which he was unable to answer at the time. But that didn't stop him from doing his utmost to find out. It was on his very first night at the loch, camped out under the stars, that Holiday experienced something that would go on to plague him on just about each and every return visit to Loch Ness. It was a dark sense of foreboding. A ghostly chill in the air. A sense of things not being quite right. Of something foul and malignant lurking just out of sight. He could practically taste it—whatever it actually was.

Holiday admitted to friends and colleagues that he always found this puzzling. After all, he had studied wildlife in Iraq, India, and Africa—and sometimes fairly dangerous wildlife, too. But there was something different about Loch Ness; something which unsettled him and smacked of the paranormal. Holiday said of this curious situation, "After sunset, Loch Ness is not a water by which to linger. The feeling is hard to define and impossible to explain ... After dark I felt that Loch Ness was better left alone."

Holiday's instinct that first night was on target. It was right at the stroke of midnight, no less, that he was suddenly awakened from his slumber by the loud tones of what sounded like huge waves pummeling the shore. He jumped up and quickly scoured the area. There was not a boat in sight that might have explained the disturbances in the water. Nor was anything else in sight. But something had clearly disturbed the loch.

It's possible that the source of the commotion showed itself to Holiday a mere two days later. That was when he was fortunate enough to encounter a monster. Dawn was breaking, and Holiday, as he scanned the waters, caught sight of something large and black breaking the surface of the loch to a height of around three feet. Then, without warning, the water churned violently and the thing plunged beneath the waves. Holiday was as excited as he was shocked. He also felt that earlier sense of foreboding overwhelm him again—much to his concern and puzzlement. Incredibly, he was of the opinion that the beast he saw was in the vicinity of forty-five feet in length. A true monster, indeed!

Despite spending untold numbers of days at Loch Ness in the months and immediate years ahead, Holiday was not to have a second encounter until 1965. Or, rather, encounters. That's right; in 1965, Holiday caught sight of a Nessie on two occasions. And both times, he was blessed with a view of the upturned, boat-like back of the beast. Incredibly, he was already formulating a theory for what the Loch Ness Monsters really were.

Welcome to the world of *Tullimonstrum gregarium*

For Ted Holiday, the plesiosaur, giant eel, and salamander theories were flawed and lacking in substance. He came to the somewhat unusual, and certainly unique, hypothesis that the Nessies were gigantic versions of everyday slugs. The biggest problem with Holiday's idea was that it was beset by issues that made it most unlikely to have merit. For example, the specific kind of invertebrate that Holiday had in mind—*Tullimonstrum*—only grew to lengths of around fourteen inches. On top of that, it lived solely in the muddy landscapes of Pennsylvania, in the United States. Oh, and one more thing that should be noted: it went extinct around three hundred million years ago. None of these seemingly important points appeared to bother Holiday in the slightest, and he continued to pursue his theory with a great deal of enthusiasm.

Such was the level of gusto that Holiday mustered, by 1968 he had written an entire book on the subject of his pet theory. Its title: *The Great Orm of Loch Ness* ("orm" being a centuries-old term meaning "worm"). There's no doubt that Holiday made a brave case for his proposal that the Nessies were massive invertebrates. The problem was that his book was entirely based on supposition and speculation. Nevertheless, he did make the valid point that whatever the Nessies might be, they were almost certainly responsible for the many and varied legends of dragons seen roaming the United Kingdom hundreds of years earlier. In that sense, Holiday believed the orms of Loch Ness were merely one colony of a creature that was far more widespread in times long gone. On that issue, he was almost certainly correct. As we have seen, Loch Ness is far from alone when it comes to the matter of monsters in the United Kingdom—the age-old sagas of the Linton Worm and the wyvern of North Wales's Llyn Cynwch Lake being famous, classic examples.

Holiday's book became a big talking point within the Nessie-seeking community. Specifically because he was positing such an unconventional scenario and, essentially, giving the middle finger to the champions of the plesiosaur, giant eel, and salamander scenarios. It was right around the time that his book was published, however, that Ted Holiday found his world turned upside down and filled to the brim with weirdness. Which was rather ironic, given just how much time and effort had gone into the writing and production of his book. And that weirdness only increased exponentially, to the point where "filled to the brim" was replaced by "absolutely overflowing."

Camera anomalies and strange synchronicity

Even though Ted Holiday sincerely believed that the *Tullimonstrum gregarium* theory had merit, he wasn't able to shake off that deep, foreboding feeling that there was something more to the Loch Ness Monsters, something which—rather paradoxically—implied they were flesh-and-blood animals but ones possessed of supernatural qualities. It was a feeling that would, ultimately, become a full-blown, unhealthy obsession, and one that pretty much dictated the rest of his short life and research.

By the time *The Great Orm of Loch Ness* was published, Holiday had not only been to the lair of the Nessies on numerous occasions, he had also had the opportunity to speak to many witnesses to the beast. In doing so, he noticed a most curious and even unsettling pattern. There were a substantial number of reports on record where eyewitnesses to the creatures had tried to photograph them, only to fail miserably. As time progressed, it became abundantly obvious to Holiday that this was not merely down to chance. When an excited soul on the shore went to grab their camera, the beast would sink beneath the waves. When someone even just thought about taking a picture, the monster would vanish below. On other occasions, cameras would malfunction. Pictures would come out blank or fogged. It was as if the Nessies were dictating, and manipulating, the situations in which the witnesses found themselves, which is exactly what Holiday came to believe was going on.

By 1969, his life was dominated by weird synchronicities—meaningful coincidences, in simple terms—which led Holiday to question both his sanity and even the very nature of reality itself. What had begun as an exciting hunt for an unknown animal was now rapidly mutating into something very different. Something dangerous and supernatural. And something which led Holiday to the very heart of Aleister Crowley's old abode, Boleskine House.

Before we get to the Holiday-Crowley issue, it's worth noting that 1968 was an important year in Nessie history for another reason. That was when Professor D. Gordon Tucker, from the University of Birmingham, England, achieved something notable at Loch Ness. He offered his help to the Loch Ness Investigation Bureau. Specifically, Tucker provided the Nessie hunters with a prototype sonar device that had the ability to sweep underwater to a distance of no less than 2,500 feet. Significantly, when deployed—at a below-surface level at Urquhart Bay's Temple Pier—the sonar tracked a number of approximately twenty-foot-long objects traveling from the lower levels of the loch to the higher levels and vice versa. They were never formally identified.

Matters of the monster variety were most definitely heating up.

15

Dragon Cults, Scorpion Men, and Dr. Dee

In June 1969, a trio of American students, who were investigating the grounds of the old cemetery that sits next to Aleister Crowley's Boleskine House, stumbled upon an ancient piece of tapestry that was wrapped around a conch (sea snail) shell. It was around four feet by five feet in size, and adorned with snake-like imagery and wording in Turkish that translated to "serpent." Interestingly, Turkey's Lake Van has a longstanding monster legend attached to it. In addition, the tapestry itself displayed pictures of lotus flowers, which, according to ancient Chinese lore, were amongst the most favored foods of the legendary dragons of old. On top of that, in China, lotus flowers were often left on the shores of lakes as offerings to the dragons that dwelled within.

One of those who had the opportunity to personally see and handle the tapestry after it was found was Ted Holiday, who had been invited to examine it. It was yet another example of the escalating and unsettling weirdness in his life. He couldn't fail to note that the tapestry was adorned with gold thread, specifically in the design of what he perceived to be thick, wormy creatures with long necks. His "great orms," no doubt. The fact that Holiday was able to determine that the tapestry lacked any mildew and wasn't even damp suggested strongly to him that it had been left there barely a day or so earlier—maybe even less than that. Possibly even just *hours* earlier. Questions put to Hal Kerr, who was the owner of Boleskine House at the time, and Richard Milne, the curator of the Inverness Museum, led nowhere, but Holiday found the whole thing highly disturbing.

The old cemetery adjacent to Boleskine House

A dragon cult and a deadly deity

It was during this period that Ted Holiday began to suspect that the discovery of the serpentine tapestry, along with the links to Boleskine House and Aleister Crowley, were indicative of a highly secret, very powerful, and maybe even deadly "dragon cult" operating in the Loch Ness area. A cult that worshiped the supernatural Nessies by night and which, perhaps, made sacrifices to the beasts under a starry, chilled sky. Possibly even *human* sacrifices—although, admittedly, there was nothing but hearsay to support this latter controversy-churning claim. Bear in mind that this was only mere months after Holiday's book, *The Great Orm of Loch Ness*, was published, which had offered a very different scenario to explain the Nessies. Life for Ted Holiday was changing at a rapid pace and in unpredictable and unsettling fashion. Who knew what might be looming around the corner? Certainly not Holiday.

The mysterious group in question, Holiday believed, were worshipers of Tiamat, a terrifying Babylonian snake goddess or sea dragon who was revered as much as she was feared—and chiefly because of her homicidal ways. She mated with Abzu, the god of fresh water, to create a number of supernatural offspring, all of dragon-like and serpent-like appearance. Then there were the dreaded Scorpion Men, equally hideous offspring of Tiamat that were, as their name suggests, a horrific combination of man and giant arachnids. As the legend goes, Abzu planned to secretly kill his children, but was thwarted from doing so when they rose up and slayed him instead. Likewise, Tiamat was ultimately slaughtered—by the god of storms, the four-eyed giant known as Marduk.

If, however, one knew the ways of the ancients, one could still call upon the power and essence of Tiamat—despite her death—as a means to achieve power, wealth, influence, and sex. Such rituals were definitively Faustian in nature, however (as they almost always are), and the conjurer had to take great heed when summoning the spirit form of Tiamat lest violent, deadly forces be unleashed. It was highly possible, thought Holiday, that the monsters seen at Loch Ness were manifestations of Tiamat, in some latter-day incarnation, and specifically provoked to manifest by that aforementioned cult.

It was situations like this that led Holiday to finally embrace the world of the occult and dismiss his previous theories and ideas on what the monsters of Loch Ness actually were. Like so many that came before him, Holiday found himself immersed in a world of the surreal, a world filled with magic—of both the black and white variety—and with devilish entities, sinister characters, and forces way beyond his control. Even beyond his understanding.

The game of the name

As an example of the eerie strangeness that soon practically dominated Holiday's every move, on one particular night in 1970—a year after the curious tapestry was found in the cemetery adjacent to Boleskine House—Holiday dined with an underwater engineer named Robert E. Love. He was a man deeply interested in the Nessie enigma. Also along for the dinner was an American friend of Love's, a Dr. M. Dee. Holiday was deeply aware of the Dr. John Dee/Edward Kelly connection to the teachings of one-time Loch Ness resident Aleister Crowley. As a result, he viewed this "game of the name" as some strange form of surreal, supernatural trickery. And, if trickery it was, it was far from over.

The American doctor came across as entirely normal and down to earth. That is, until the night came to a close. As the atmosphere took on a menacing nature, Dee leaned forward and whispered to Holiday that he had an ancestor of that same name, one who lived during the period when Queen Elizabeth I reigned. This was clearly a reference to John Dee, colleague of the occultist Edward Kelly. The doctor knew this, he added, because he had spent much of his time in England researching his family tree. Whether or not his words were meant as a warning for Holiday to keep his nose out of things that didn't concern him was never made clear, but

Holiday most certainly took it that way. And the Dee connections didn't end there.

One day in 1971, Holiday was scouring the loch in the Achnahannet area when he suddenly noticed the yellowy form of three letters in the water. They were a D, an E, and one more E: *Dee*. They were caused by yellow subsoil that had fallen into the loch as a bulldozing crew worked to widen the stretch of road on which Holiday was standing. For Holiday, this simply could not have been down to chance, even though he tried to convince himself that was exactly the truth of the matter. Hardly surprisingly, he was plunged into ever-deepening paranoia. Unfortunately, he never really escaped from its clutches, and his descent into the domain of the supernatural Nessies was well and truly cemented.

We now must take a brief diversion to another Scottish loch with a monster tradition. As for why, specifically, we're going to do this, consider that in the 1968–1969 period—when Ted Holiday found himself immersed in weirdness, dragon cults, paranormal phenomena, and soon Dr. Dee—there was a sudden wave of sightings of a certain cousin of the Nessies. A coincidence? Doubtful. *Extremely* doubtful.

Morag the monster

Make mention of Scottish lake monsters to most people and it will inevitably conjure up imagery of the world's most famous unknown water beast, the Loch Ness Monster. As we have seen in relation to the matter of the deadly kelpie, however, there are more than a few Scottish lakes with legends of diabolical creatures attached to them. While many of the accounts are decidedly fragmentary in nature, that is not always the case. Welcome to the world of Morag, the resident beastie of Loch Morar, which decided to put on several spectacular displays in 1968 and 1969—the very time when seriously weird stuff was afoot at Loch Ness and Ted Holiday found his life and research in a whirl.

At just over eleven and a half miles in length and located near the western coast of Scotland, Loch Morar has the distinction of being the deepest body of fresh water in the British Isles, with a depth of slightly more than one thousand feet. Unlike Loch Ness, the water of which is almost black, Loch Morar can boast of having practically clear water. It takes its name from the village of Morar, which is situated near the western end of the loch and is known for being the site of the Battle of Morar in 1602—a violent, death-filled confrontation between the Mackenzie and MacDonell clans.

As for the monster Morag, the tales are many. What makes them so different from the ones coming out of Loch Ness, however, is not the descriptions of the creatures, but that the reports are often hard to uncover. Unlike Loch Ness, Loch Morar is an isolated, seldom-visited loch. It is bereft of much in the way of a large population, and it is not particularly easy to access. The result: tourists to Scotland very rarely visit it. The same goes for native Scots, too! For that reason, just like with Las Vegas, what happens at Loch Morar is very often destined to stay there. Nevertheless, there are enough classic cases on record to strongly suggest that very strange things lurk in Loch Morar.

A catalog of creatures

Alexander Carmichael, a main contributor to Campbell's *Popular Tales of the West Highlands*, penned the following description of the beast: "The Morag dwells in Loch Morar. She gives her name to the lake and still appears when any of the old Macdonalds of Morar die. Like the other water deities she is half human half fish. The lower portion of her body is in the form of a grilse and the upper in the form of a small woman of highly developed breasts with long flowing yellow hair falling down her snow white back and breast. She is represented as being fair, beautiful and very timid and never seen save when one of the Morar family dies or when the clan falls in battle."

The fact that Carmichael termed the Morag "half human half fish," while others have described it as definitively serpentine, is a good indicator that, like the kelpies of Loch Ness, the Morags were shapeshifters.

One of the earliest reports of a Morag came from a man named James McDonald, who claimed a sighting of a three-humped creature snaking through the waters of Loch Morar late one cold, dark night in January 1887. Rather ominously, superstitious locals perceived this as a distinctly ill omen: the three sections of the beast were seen as death, a coffin, and a grave—such was the fear that the villagers had of the monster in their midst. Eight years later, Sir Theodore Henry Brinckman, 2nd Baronet, and his wife were fishing at the loch when a long thing, shaped like an upturned boat, surfaced from the depths. One of the locals, a man named MacLaren, dismissed the matter as nothing more than a sighting of the loch's resident monster. His casual tones suggest he saw nothing strange about a huge beast roaming the length, breadth, and depth of the loch.

An astonishing sighting occurred in 1948, when a man named Alexander MacDonnell sighted one of the Morags actually on the shore at Bracorina Point. Within a few moments, it practically belly-flopped into the water and vanished. It was a beast described as the size of an elephant. Needless to say, there is no known indigenous creature in the British Isles that rivals an elephant in size. In the same year, a number of people, led by a Mr. John Gillies, caught sight of an approximately thirty-foot-long animal displaying no less than four humps.

Then, in August 1968, John MacVarish had a very close view of an unknown animal in Loch Morar, one that displayed a snake-like head of about six feet in length and had very dark or black skin. But without doubt the most amazing—and, for the witnesses, nerve-wracking—encounters occurred on the night of August 16, 1969. That was when William Simpson and Duncan McDonnell were traveling on the waters, near the west end of the loch. Suddenly, as if out of nowhere, a large animal—possibly thirty feet in length—loomed into view and actually collided with their motorboat. Or perhaps "rammed it" would be a better term to use. When Simpson tried to blast the creature with his shotgun, it sank beneath the waves—as a result of the ear-splitting sound of the gun, both men concluded, rather than as a result of Simpson having actually shot the monster.

This occurred just two months after Ted Holiday had investigated the discovery of the strange, serpent-themed tapestry in the old cemetery that sits next to Boleskine House. A tapestry designed to raise terrible lake monsters. It may well have done so. Not just at Loch Ness, but at Loch Morar, too.

Now, on to the 1970s and back to Loch Ness.

16

UFOs, a Movie, a Conspiracy, and a Rock Star

The seventies began in appropriately weird fashion for the Loch Ness Monster: 1970 was the year in which a big-bucks movie was made by the acclaimed film director Billy Wilder. Its title was *The Private Life of Sherlock Holmes*. It starred Robert Stephens as the world's most famous private detective and Colin Blakely as his sidekick, Dr. Watson. It was a movie that saw the dynamic duo, in the course of pursuing the mysterious disappearance of a Belgian engineer, ending up on the waters of Loch Ness—along with the wife of said Belgian engineer—and confronting the monster itself. Well, in a fashion, at least.

The "monster" of the movie was actually an ingeniously created submarine, supposedly designed and built by the British military to resemble a sea creature in the event someone might see it during its nighttime testing—specifically, German spies suspected of being in the area. I mention all of this because the movie prop for the monster-submarine plays a significant role in the real hunt for Nessie, as will become clear in the next chapter. Remember, too, that Nessie and a submarine (albeit a toy one) were integral parts of the 1934 hoaxing of the so-called "Surgeon's Photograph."

Before we move on, it's worth noting that there is a curious piece of high-level conspiracy attached to Billy Wilder's movie. And to Wilder himself. Shortly after the tumultuous events of the Second World War came to a close in 1945, Wilder was commissioned to make a documentary, titled *Death Mills*, on the grim subject of the terrible atrocities the Nazis inflicted on the Jews during the war. The commission came from the U.S. Department of War's Psychological Warfare Department (PWD).

It's interesting to note that the PWD has been linked—at rumor level, at least—with the controversial story of an American lake monster known as Paddler, reportedly the giant serpentine denizen of Lake Pend Oreille, Idaho. An American equivalent of Nessie, one might be justified in saying. Or quite possibly not. On a visit to the lake, I discovered that there were longstanding murmurings among the locals that the PWD deliberately created the stories of Paddler in the 1940s—which is when sightings of the beast first began—to deflect people away from something else: namely, the testing of secret mini-submarines in the lake. As the story goes, the PWD hoped that if someone happened to inadvertently see one of the mini-subs briefly break the surface of the lake, they would assume it was Paddler. Thus a secret submarine would remain ingeniously hidden from Nazi or Japanese agents under a cloak and camouflage of the monster variety.

Of course, this is precisely the scenario played out in *The Private Life of Sherlock Holmes*—whose writer and director, Billy Wilder, twenty-five years earlier just happened to work with the PWD—the very people who had created a monster ruse in Lake Pend Oreille. Almost certainly, Wilder was quietly told of this bizarre and wonderful piece of Second World War–era deception by PWD staff, and then decided to make it the centerpiece of his Holmes and Watson movie a quarter of a century later. Precisely what the highest echelons of the U.S. military thought, when they saw their peculiar 1940s-era program at Lake Pend Oreille fictionalized and transplanted to the heart of Loch Ness in 1970, remains unknown.

In that sense, the secrets of Loch Ness are not just of the supernatural kind. They are of the conspiratorial type, too. Could the Loch Ness Monster saga get any weirder? Yes, it could. And, it does.

Move over, Nessie; the aliens are coming

On August 13, 1971, a notable encounter occurred at Loch Ness. Not with a monster, but with a UFO! The witness was one Graham Snape, who told Ted Holiday that he saw an unidentified object crossing the skies above Loch Ness in a left-to-right fashion, quickly, and with not even a bit of accompanying noise. The somewhat circular-shaped UFO was purple with a white center. By his own admission, Snape was unsure of the size of the object but suggested it was around five feet in diameter.

Holiday was, by now, so deep into the world of the paranormal that Snape's report scarcely phased him in the slightest. Snape's encounter, however, was nothing compared to what occurred just three days later. It was something that practically preempted, by six years, the final segment of Steven Spielberg's 1977 movie *Close Encounters of the Third Kind*, in which aliens make face-to-face contact with the human race.

E. T. in the woods

Jan-Ove Sundberg, a twenty-three-year-old Swede, recounts that he was in a section of woodland above Foyers Bay on August 14, 1971, at some point between 8:30 and 9:30 a.m., when he came across something staggering. No, not a fully grown Nessie roaming the landscape in a fashion akin to the beast seen by Lieutenant McP Fordyce in April 1932; rather, Sundberg near-stumbled upon a landed UFO and its presumed extraterrestrial crew! The craft was situated in a clearing, giving the impression that its pilots had chosen the site deliberately as it gave them the opportunity to land and hide their presence—that is, until Sundberg inadvertently foiled their plan.

The craft was, to say the least, a decidedly odd one. It was around thirty feet in length, dark gray in color, and cigar-shaped. It had a significantly sized section on top that reminded Sundberg of a large handle. The overall image was that of a giant iron used for getting the creases out of clothing. Sundberg's amazement turned to concern when, out of the trees, came a trio of figures: all humanoid in shape, of approximately human proportions, and dressed in outfits that closely resembled the outfits worn by divers. In fact, at first, Sundberg assumed they *were* divers, from a then-active team that was searching the depths of Loch Ness for the monster. However, it became apparent the three were not divers when they entered the odd-looking craft via a panel and the craft took to the skies, vertically, for about sixty feet. After which it began to move horizontally, over the hills, in the direction of nearby Loch Mhor.

Further photographic problems at Loch Ness

Ted Holiday made what was, perhaps, an inevitable observation about the Sundberg affair. As mentioned previously, he had perceived a pattern in which the Nessies were able to thwart photos and photographers. Curiously, but typically, if someone at Loch Ness was confronted by something incredible and mysterious, they were forthwith highly unlikely to be able to secure photographic evidence of its existence. Sundberg explained this phenomenon, however, by stating that he had felt a sense of paralysis came over him.

Actually, Sundberg did manage to take just one photo, but it was one which researcher Stuart Campbell came to believe showed nothing unusual. Indeed, it's important to note that Campbell believed Sundberg's sighting to have been nothing but a strange form of hallucination—which, inevitably, means we have to be very careful how, and to what extent, we choose to embrace the case. Whatever the answer, it's intriguing that Sundberg claimed on his return to Sweden that he was threatened by Men in Black, experienced supernatural events in his home—such as poltergeist activity—and received odd phone calls. Three years later, Ted Holiday had his very own supernaturally themed Men in Black encounter at Loch Ness, as will soon be demonstrated.

Going back to the matter of that curious paralysis which reportedly prevented Sundberg from capturing close-up imagery of the craft and crew of the UFO, the husband-and-wife team of Colin and Janet Bord have, like Holiday, noted that camera-based problems have always been issues for Nessie-seekers; in fact, this has been a problem since the very year in which mega-scale Nessie fever began. The Bords say, "When Hugh Gray took the now famous photograph of the Loch Ness Monster on 12 November 1933 he did in fact take five shots but four were blank."

The inference is obvious: there is some force at work, both in and around Loch Ness, that prevents people from getting too close to the truth of the things they so intensely seek. And it prevents them in what is clearly a toying, manipulative fashion. Maybe even in a cruel and malevolent fashion.

Finally on this case, we have something rather synchronistic. August 1971, the month of Sundberg's UFO encounter, was the very same month that I traveled to Loch Ness for the first time, as a six-year-old, with my parents. It was the height of the regular summer holidays. And, with the UK's schools closed for a customary period of six weeks, it allowed us to spend much welcome time at the water's edge. Although I saw nothing strange on August 14, and neither did my parents, it was a life-changing experience—one that eventually set me on a quest for the truth surrounding the Nessies. It would be appropriately weird, and weirdly appropriate, if a young Nick Redfern was unknowingly in the presence of both monsters *and* aliens—the former lurking in the loch, the latter hiding in the surrounding trees.

"Bad vibes" and a beheading

Yet another infamous development occurred at Loch Ness in 1971. That was the year in which Led Zeppelin guitarist, Jimmy Page, purchased Aleister Crowley's old abode, Boleskine House. Ironically for someone who was a major devotee and follower of the teachings of Crowley, Page actually spent very little time at the house—which may not have been a bad thing for the rock star, considering everything that had gone on there previously. Indeed, as we have seen, Boleskine House has a long and turbulent history. Despite his lack of time spent at Crowley's old home, Page certainly acknowledged that the entire place was saturated in high-strangeness. In a 1975 *Rolling Stone* interview, he said it had "bad vibes," adding that "a man was beheaded there and sometimes you can hear his head rolling down."

None of this kept Page away from the world of the occult. That much is evidenced by the fact that he later owned a famous London bookshop devoted to all things supernatural, paranormal, and esoteric. Its name: The Equinox. In addition, portions of Led Zeppelin's movie, *The Song Remains the Same* (released in 1976 but shot in 1973), were filmed on the grounds of Boleskine House. Page sold the creepy old house in 1992.

Little did anyone know it at the time, but in 1972—one year after the Sundberg encounter—the story of the creatures of Loch Ness reached near-unparalleled levels.

17

Plesiosaurs that Weren't

The biggest development in the story of the Loch Ness Monster—post-1933, that is—occurred in 1972. That was when a couple of astonishing photographs surfaced that added much weight to the theories of those who believed the Nessies to be plesiosaurs. It was all thanks to a Dr. Robert Rines, President of the Academy of Applied Science in Boston, Massachusetts. Rines was also a skilled musician and composer, and someone who worked in the field of law. He had a BS from the Massachusetts Institute of Technology and a PhD from National Chiao Tung University, Taiwan.

It all began in the waters off Urquhart Castle on August 7, 1972, and continued into the early hours of August 8. Rines and his colleagues were onboard a boat and recorded something remarkable on their Raytheon sonar equipment. The sonar was anchored at around 35 or 36 feet and some object, or creature, was perhaps ten feet below it. As for its size, the sonar readings suggested something in the order of twenty to thirty feet in length. On top of that, a large number of fish seemingly fled the area in question right at the time the sonar recorded the presence of the large whatever-it-was. The device was rigged to take photos every fifteen seconds, which was most fortuitous, since the camera seemingly caught nothing less than the near-pristine image of a large, plesiosaur-like flipper and a portion of the body to which it was attached.

The Legend of Nessie website says, more specifically, that "the picture obtained, although indistinct due to the murkiness of the water, shows the offside hind quarter, flipper and part of the tail of a large animal with a rough textured skin of a greeny-brown color." Too good to be true? Well, let's see.

"Incongruous shadow features which I cannot explain"

Darren Naish is a respected paleontologist and someone with a deep interest in cryptozoology. Naish is someone who not only doubts the veracity of the Rines photos, but who is very vocal in his belief that they are fakes. Naish's words are not without foundation. It's now known that, at the absolute very least, the images were—to put it diplomatically—manipulated and enhanced. It's important to note that Naish is no debunker. Rather, he is someone who has an open mind on the matter of cryptids and their possible existence, but who has studied the Rines pictures carefully and concluded they are sorely lacking in credibility.

Naish's comments are paralleled by the words of Dick Raynor, who was one of the people aboard the boat on the night of August 7–8, 1972. Raynor says something that, in a fashion which leaves no room for interpretation, contradicts the story that so many have heard and so dearly want to believe: "The enhanced 'flipper' photographs show incongruous shadow features which I cannot explain other than as deliberate artistic improvement, i.e. 'retouching.'"

Those who faithfully adhere to the notion that the Nessies are flesh-and-blood animals, and possibly plesiosaurs, should take care-

ful note of the words of Raynor. He was, after all, one of the key players in the story, on-site and onboard at the time, and someone with
no motivation whatsoever to denounce the imagery without a good
reason. His words offer a solid, fact-based explanation for why the
pictures do not, and cannot, show what they appear to show: a flesh-
and-blood animal of the plesiosaur variety.

It's interesting to note that Sir Peter Scott and Robert Rines
used these photos as the basis for a new name for the Nessies: *Nes-*
siteras rhombopteryx, which just happens to be an anagram of "Monster hoax by Sir Peter S." That could, however, be nothing more
than an extraordinary coincidence, since *Nessiteras rhombopteryx* is
also an anagram of "Yes, both pix are monsters, R."

Rines caused an equally big stir in 1975 when he secured even
more fantastic and controversial images, one of which seemed to
show a gargoyle-like head and the other the head, neck, body, and
limbs of what does look very much like a plesiosaur. It has been
suggested, however, that the head is either a tree stump or the head
of the prop monster-submarine used in Billy Wilder's 1970 movie,
The Private Life of Sherlock Holmes. Unknown to even many Nessie
enthusiasts is the fact that during the filming of the movie, the life-
sized model head and neck of the "monster" unfortunately sank beneath the waves of Loch Ness and was never recovered—something
which makes it not at all implausible that an occasional underwater
photo of an assumed Nessie head might actually be a photo of the
carefully crafted creation of special effects experts. As for the plesiosaur-like body imagery secured by Rines, Darren Naish suggests
that our old buddy, pareidolia—the brain's attempt to interpret and
transform random imagery into something more—was the culprit.

The Rines photos led many to conclude that the Loch Ness Monsters were real, flesh-and-blood, breathing animals. It wasn't long, however, before Ted Holiday was back on the scene, pursuing with vigor the occult aspects of the puzzle.

18

Exorcising the Monster

On the night of June 2, 1973, Loch Ness played host to something truly extraordinary. It was nothing less than a full-blown exorcism, one that was designed to forever banish the malignant monsters from the deep and dark waters. It was all the work of Donald Omand, both a doctor and a reverend. He was a man who had substantial knowledge on, and experience of, the domain of all things supernatural. Of his thoughts on the Nessie phenomenon, Omand said, "Each year I drive along most of the long, somewhat tedious, shore of Loch Ness in traveling from the Kyle of Lochalsh to Inverness, and never yet have I observed the monster."

We should not, however, interpret this to mean that Omand was a skeptic when it came to the Loch Ness creatures. In fact, quite the opposite is the case. He believed that one had to be at the loch at the right time to encounter one of the monsters. His reasoning was simple: the Nessies are supernatural entities that can only be encountered when the circumstances are conducive to an encounter. For Omand, the monsters were projections of something large and terrifying from a bygone era—monsters that may have existed millions of years ago but which continue to manifest, albeit in paranormal form.

For the god-fearing reverend, the supernatural beasts had to be cast out, and the sooner the better, too. He was helped in his venture by none other than Ted Holiday. Holiday's interests in Omand's opinions on the monsters of Loch Ness were prompted by the latter's book *Experiences of a Present Day Priest*. It's a book that details the reverend's nagging and worrying suspicions that lake monsters have supernatural rather than physical origins. Omand was someone who had also focused his attentions on combating black magic and witchcraft, and had even exorcised bears, lions, and tigers believed to be in the throes of dark, demonic possession. He was, then, hardly your average priest. But he was exactly the kind of priest needed to rid Loch Ness of its strange inhabitants.

The church's monster hunter

It's worth noting how, and why, the Reverend Donald Omand became so deeply immersed in the Loch Ness Monster controversy. In 1967, he had his own sighting of a black-humped beast in Loch Long, which is located to the south, in Argyll & Bute, Scotland. It was only in view for mere moments, but even so it was enough time for Omand to have gotten a clear look at it and to realize it wasn't anything so simple as a wave or a rotting tree trunk. It was a monster—and it was a monster that seemingly had the ability to boil and bubble the water.

Omand was further exposed to the mysteries of water monsters in the following year, 1968—the very same year in which Ted Holiday was coming around to the idea that the Nessies had supernatural origins. Omand had confided in a friend what he had seen at Loch Long in 1967. That friend was a Norwegian sailor named Jan Andersen. The upshot of this revelation was that Captain Andersen invited Omand to accompany him, in June 1968, on a trip through the Fjord of the Trolls, otherwise known as the "eeriest waterway in

Norway." Omand jumped at the opportunity. Had he known what was going to happen, he might have declined the invite.

The pair negotiated the mysterious waters, and just like at Loch Long one year earlier, the water began to boil and bubble. As if right on cue, a pair of large, dark-colored humps rose from the depths and headed directly for Andersen's boat. Such was the size of the humps, Omand was deeply afraid that the leviathan might actually capsize the vessel and send the pair to Davy Jones's locker.

It was not to be, however. Captain Andersen reassured Omand that the animal would bring no harm to them. Sure enough, at the last moment the creature abruptly changed course and sank beneath the surface. Andersen stressed to Omand the importance of recognizing that although the monster did no physical harm, it was definitively malevolent. Puzzled as to how the monster could be considered evil when the pair was not hurt, Omand was told by Andersen that such creatures did not bring physical harm to anyone, as they wished to be perceived as being nonmalevolent. This, however, was nothing more than a cunning and callous ruse. Omand asked Andersen what he meant by that, and the seafarer replied that it was not the bodies of witnesses that the creatures were set on disrupting, but their minds and characters—to the point of provoking anxiety, paranoia, and, finally, mental collapse.

An investigation into the totally fantastic

Ted Holiday could personally relate to Andersen's writings, given how his own mindset had been radically altered and manipulated by exposure to the Nessies. He wasted no time in sending Omand a letter, applauding him on his train of thought. It was the letter and the praise which led Omand to invite Holiday to spend a weekend with him at his home in Devon, England. Holiday didn't need to be asked twice: he jumped at the opportunity. During the course of their monster-themed meeting, Holiday learned that Omand had already spoken with the Bishop of Crediton about performing an exorcism at Loch Ness—which the bishop thought was an excellent idea. In light of his dramatic change of opinion on the nature of the lake monsters of Loch Ness, Holiday thought it would be a very wise move, too.

Yet he had another reason for contacting Omand: 1973 marked the publication of Holiday's second book on lake monsters, *The Dragon and the Disc*. Holiday gave his book just about the most relevant and applicable subtitle possible: *An investigation into the totally fantastic*. It was in the pages of *The Dragon and the Disc* that Holiday finally said goodbye to his earlier, and far more down-to-earth, theories for the things of Loch Ness. His new book encompassed not just the paranormal side of lake monsters in general, and the Nessies in particular, but UFOs in times both ancient and modern. He also dwelled on that curiously synchronistic series of events that spanned 1969 to 1971 and which were focused around Aleister Crowley, Boleskine House, that unsettling dragon cult, and Dr. John Dee and his modern-day, slightly sinister relative.

And, so, keeping all this in mind, Holiday set a date to meet with Reverend Omand, the one man who, more than any other, shared his deep conviction that the Loch Ness Monsters were not what they seemed to be. They were worse. Much, much worse. And now it was time to confront them. Maybe even head-on.

"I felt a distinct tension creep into the atmosphere at this point"

A decision was reached to undertake a number of exorcisms: several on the shore at various points along the loch, and one in the dead center, on the water itself. A small boat was generously provided by Wing Commander Basil Cary, who lived with his wife near the shore of the loch and was particularly intrigued by the monster legend. The BBC was intrigued, too, and determined to be on the scene to capture the exorcism on camera—or, as it transpired, a re-creation of the exorcism, since the camera crew turned up late.

As things began, the seriousness of the affair quickly became apparent. When the pair arrived at Lochend—along with Tony Artus, a captain in the British Army who had an interest in the controversy of Nessie, and a photographer friend of Omand— Omand asked them to kneel, which they did, and holy water was sprinkled on their foreheads, in the shape of a cross. As if right on cue, a chilled wind suddenly enveloped the area. That was not necessarily a good sign—at all. With that act performed, Omand approached the mysterious waters, lowered his head, and said in quiet and deliberate tones:

"I exorcise thee, O Creature of Salt, by the living God, by the true God, by the Holy God, by that God who by the prophet Eliseus commanded thee to be cast into the water to cure its barrenness: that thou mayest by this exorcism be made beneficial to the faithful, and become to all those who make use of thee healthful both to soul and body: and that in whatsoever place thou shalt be sprinkled, all illusions and wickedness and crafty wiles of Satan may be chased away and depart from that place; and every unclean spirit commanded in His name, who is to come to judge the living and the dead and the world by fire."

It was quite a statement, to be sure! Omand continued, asking for Loch Ness and its surroundings to be free of malevolent, supernatural spirits, and that the monsters be forever dispatched to a paranormal realm far away from the loch. Just for good measure, Omand sprinkled a liberal amount of holy water into the loch. The same ritual was undertaken, and the same words were spoken, at a pebbled stretch of beach at Borlum Bay, and at Fort Augustus.

These particular exorcisms had a profound effect on Ted Holiday. Looking back on that night a few years later, he said that while he held no particular, firm beliefs when it came to the matter of religion, "I felt a distinct tension creep into the atmosphere at this point. It was as if we had shifted some invisible levers, and were awaiting the result."

In addition, Holiday recalled that the photographer who was present looked very worried. Tony Artus had plunged into a state of complete silence. Only the reverend seemed unaffected by the near-unique situation all four found themselves in. By the time the final land-based exorcism was over, evening was nearing its end and the all-enveloping darkness of night was beginning to blanket the area. There was no time to waste: the intrepid mariners headed for the waters of Fort Augustus, intent on bringing the matter of Nessie's presence to a hopeful closure. Whitecaps and a howling wind appeared, seemingly out of nowhere. Yet again, it appeared, a bad sign was the order of the day—or, rather, of the night. Holiday felt a distinct air of menace envelope him and he took a deep breath. If there be monsters, now was possibly the time for them to make their presence known and engage the reverend in the ultimate battle of good vs. evil. Once again, the reverend had words to say—and to say out loud—as he called for the reign of the monsters to end and for their banishing from Loch Ness.

The last of the holy water was then poured into the loch, amid hopes that it would help to drive the paranormal presence away for good. Instead, something else happened: the Reverend Omand visibly and suddenly paled, shivered, and appeared close to passing out. The group raced to get the boat to the shore, and there then followed a torturously slow walk across the surrounding, now-darkness-filled, hills. It was a walk that saw Holiday and Tony Artus constantly supporting Omand to prevent him from keeling over into the grass. Despite the seemingly serious nature of the situation, Omand later explained that feeling drained and light-headed were two of the classic after-effects of performing an exorcism, hence nothing to overly worry about.

After a while, the reverend was fully recovered and the group retired to their beds, earnestly hoping and praying that the Nessies would never again darken Loch Ness. As history has shown, however, they did—time and time again.

The powers of evil hit back

Perhaps as some form of malignant backlash against the valiant attempts to banish the monsters, dark forces seemed to hover ominously around the area for almost a week afterwards. Several days after the exorcism, Holiday took a nighttime drive to the home of Basil and Winifred Cary, specifically to get their views on the Sundberg UFO encounter at Loch Ness in August 1971. As a psychic with notable powers of precognition, and someone who had spent time in India and worked for the Special Operations Executive during the Second World War, Mrs. Cary was not someone who encouraged delving into the domain of the unknown. She did her utmost to *discourage* it.

As Holiday brought up the matter of the UFO encounter, Mrs. Cary's face took on a deeply furrowed frown, then a look of concern, and finally one of downright fear. In no uncertain terms, she quietly cautioned Holiday to keep away from the reported landing site of the allegedly alien craft, warning him that the only outcome of such an action would be disaster—or worse.

An evil presence was apparently hovering around and listening intently to her words. At that very moment, a whirlwind-like sound filled the air, shadowy and racing forms filled the garden, and heavy thumping sounds reverberated around the old property. A plume of a black, smoke-like substance appeared amid the garden's flowers and plants. An ear-splitting scream from Mrs. Cary filled the living room. The entire household was briefly enveloped by a cloak of terror and mayhem. After around twenty seconds or so, however, normality returned and the brief atmosphere of paranormal terror was gone. For a while, anyway. In fact, for less than a day.

Ted Holiday was about to encounter something arguably even worse than a Loch Ness Monster.

19

A Confrontation with a Man in Black

As dawn broke on the following morning, Holiday took a walk down to the loch. What a catastrophic mistake that was. As he did so, he could not fail to see a man, at a distance of around ninety feet, standing atop the slope that led directly down to Loch Ness. This was no normal man, however. It may not even have been a man at all. Whoever—or *whatever*—this curious character was, he was dressed entirely in black from head to toe. Whereas most people who go to Loch Ness focus their attentions on the deep waters, in the hope they just might be lucky enough to see something monstrous rear its head, this character had his back to the loch and was staring directly at Holiday ... who later commented, in his book *The Goblin Universe*, that as the figure focused on him, "I felt a strong sensation of malevolence, cold and passionless."

The man appeared to be dressed in what Holiday described as black plastic. His hands were gloved (black, too), and his head was covered by something that looked like a motorcycle helmet. No surprises on its color. Goggles covered his eyes, and even his nose and mouth were covered—by a black band, possibly made of cloth. Holiday tentatively walked towards the definitive Man in

Black. The MIB neither moved nor acknowledged his presence. Most terrifying of all, there appeared to be no eyes behind the goggles.

Shocked, Holiday continued walking for about ten feet and then stopped. It was his quickly thought-out intention to pretend to fall on the grass and reach out to the man for support as he did so—specifically to see if the man was physical in form or some kind of intangible specter. He was prevented from doing so, however, when the sounds of whistling and unintelligible whisperings filled the air, and the MIB vanished—as in dematerialized, literally. As Holiday—now petrified out of his wits—shakily scanned the half a mile of open road that dominated the landscape, it became clear to him that there was simply no way the man could have made good a stealthy escape in conventional fashion. Stunned to his core, he tried to reconcile the whole thing as nothing but a bizarre hallucination—a theory that, he knew deep down, simply wasn't viable.

Holiday tried to take his mind off the matter by paying a last visit to the Cary family and going to say his goodbyes to the Reverend Omand. It was all to no avail; the specter of the thing in black remained, like an albatross around his neck.

Another encounter involving a Man in Black

Of equal fascination, and of deep relevance to this story, is the fact that back in September 1866, there occurred the sighting of a mournful-looking man, in black attire, on the hills near Lochindorb. A terrified farmer saw him strapped to the back of a large, fiendish dog that was prowling the hills. The beast had a bit and a bridle in its mouth, which instantly provokes recollections of the story of Willox the Warlock and how he stole a bit and bridle from the kelpie he fought. The farmer in Lochindorb didn't wait around to see what might happen next—he fled the hills for the safety of his home, fearful that the shapeshifting kelpie-hound might wish to make him its next victim. It was probably a very wise move. Can it be mere coincidence that two encounters—separated by a time span of more than one hundred years, it should be noted—both had Man in Black components to them? I strongly suggest that no, it *cannot* be a coincidence.

There is a decidedly sinister sequel to this aspect of Ted Holiday's quest for the truth of the Loch Ness Monster and his Man in Black experience. One year later, in 1974, Holiday's creature-seeking excursions were suddenly cut short by a serious heart attack—right at the very spot where the MIB had manifested and then vanished around twelve months earlier. A warning, perhaps, to Holiday that he should walk away from the matter of the Loch Ness Monster. And walk away *now*—while he still had the chance, and before the reaper came calling for his very mind and soul.

Beware of the Men in Black

For most people, any mention of the Men in Black conjures up imagery of the dark-suited secret agents portrayed by Will Smith and Tommy Lee Jones of the blockbuster movie series. The reality of the situation is far stranger, however. There is *zero* evidence that the MIB have any connections to agencies of government, the military, or the intelligence community—of any nation. Rather, there is strong evidence to show that the Men in Black are of occult origins.

One of the first people exposed to the Men in Black was a UFO researcher from Bridgeport, Connecticut, named Albert Bender. When, in the early 1950s, Bender began to dabble—and dabble recklessly—in the world of the supernatural, he was visited by three men dressed in black who materialized in his bedroom amid a foul odor of devilish brimstone. Then there are reports of the MIB threatening users of Ouija boards. The Men in Black have vampire-like parallels: they generally surface only at night; their skin is milk-white in color; they will not enter a person's home until they are specifically invited to do so. And they have the highly disturbing ability to drain people of energy—mirroring the old legends of black-garbed vampires draining unwary souls of their blood while they slept.

There seems to be little doubt that the foul thing Ted Holiday encountered on that fateful morning was a definitive example of a supernatural MIB. And on the matter of that menacing Man in Black ...

Psychomania, George Sanders, and Boleskine House

Recall how, in 1972, a former owner of Boleskine House, the British actor George Sanders, committed suicide. His last film, released the following year, was *Psychomania*—which is, without any doubt whatsoever, one of the oddest movies of the undead ever made. Filmed in the United Kingdom in 1972, *Psychomania* stars Nicky Henson and was directed by Don Sharp, who was responsible for such movies as *Kiss of the Vampire* and *The Curse of the Fly*.

The plot line revolves around the actions of a motorcycle gang that call themselves The Living Dead. They have the name emblazoned prominently on the back of their black leather jackets, and they spend much of their time hanging out at the Seven Witches: a small, Stonehenge-like, Bronze Age circle of ancient standing stones that feature heavily in the movie. Using the directions of an ancient supernatural ritual, one by one the gang members kill themselves. They don't stay dead, however. They rise from the grave and go on murderous sprees. With its almost dreamlike qualities that border on the psychedelic and its focus on old stone circles and ancient rituals, Don Sharp's *Psychomania* has attained cult-like status amongst horror and undead aficionados.

Most important of all in this odd state of affairs is that Ted Holiday's "Biker in Black," with his helmet and goggles, sounds very much like the fictional, risen-from-the-grave bikers of *Psychomania*—a movie made one year before Holiday's unsettling encounter with the MIB and starring a soon-to-be victim of suicide, George Sanders, who owned Loch Ness's most infamous abode, Aleister Crowley's Boleskine House. What goes around apparently comes around at Loch Ness. And it does so in deadly fashion.

Seriously Strange

Finally for 1973, on June 9 of that year a man named Steve Corzula and a diver friend, from the University Marine Biological Station, Millport, arranged to meet with Ted Holiday to share the details of a curious tale. The pair had been diving near Loch Ness's Aldourie pier on Easter Saturday when they found "half a dozen or more dome-shaped hummocks of hard sand and stones about 3–4 feet high and 20 feet in diameter," as Holiday later recounted. This in just around thirty feet of water.

This just added to the list of very weird events that Holiday was hearing of or experiencing: the Nessies, UFO encounters, demonic activity, exorcisms, and now what seemed to be a burial site dating from the Bronze Age. Let's not ignore the fact that in *Pyschomania*, the standing stones known as the Seven Witches date from the Bronze Age. In a decidedly odd way, fact was spilling over into the world of fiction. And vice-versa.

Things would get even stranger in 1976 (as we'll see in chapter 21), when yet more ancient archaeological structures were found in Loch Ness—structures which may have had direct links to the presence of the monsters in centuries past. Before we get to that, however, it's time to see how even Tim Dinsdale—who had championed the idea that the Nessies were unknown but real animals—found himself heading down a supernatural road.

20

The Supernatural Nessie
and *Dr. Who*

Nineteen-seventy-four was a year in which Tim Dinsdale made a notable, but carefully and tactfully worded, statement to Ted Holiday on the paranormal connections to the mystery of the Loch Ness beasts. As far as the monster-hunting community of the day was concerned, Dinsdale was firmly and forever in the flesh-and-blood category when it came to the nature of the creatures of the loch. Many within that community are *still* of that opinion today; chiefly because they are unaware of what was going on behind the scenes. "Firmly" and "forever," however, are far too rigid and incorrect words to use. Privately, Disndale had a sneaking suspicion that something else was very possibly afoot, even if he preferred to not overly broadcast his views publicly. While Dinsdale's large-scale silence on the matter of the supernatural aspects of the Nessie controversy may be understandable to some, it also smacks of a man unsure of himself and lacking the strength of character to say, publicly, what he really thought. Or, at the very least, what he suspected.

In April 1974—in a private reply to a letter that Holiday had sent to him describing the most recent weirdness at the loch, including the exorcism and the creepy Man in Black affair—Dinsdale had some notable things to say. He admitted to Holiday that he had crossed paths with what appeared to be a paranormal component to the mystery of the monsters of Loch Ness, but remained baffled regarding how something of a supernatural nature could provoke such things as wakes in the water, photos, and sonar recordings.

"It was as though some awful influence pervaded the atmosphere. Something evil."

It's very instructive to note that Tim Dinsdale's thoughts on the supernatural theory for the Nessies went right back to 1965, which was only a few short years after his much-championed film footage was secured. In September of that year, Dinsdale traveled to the loch for the ninth time, with the hope of securing high-resolution imagery of the creatures—specifically from the south shore, east of Foyers Bay. But it very nearly proved to be his *final* visit to those notorious waters. Indeed, his trip was plagued by an extraordinary amount of escalating disasters. His small boat was capsized. He was quickly laid low by a viral infection. He suffered repeated problems with his electrical equipment (something that is often reported in both UFO-themed and Bigfoot-themed encounters). And he badly damaged one of his hands, almost losing the tip of one of his fingers in the process.

Some might put this catalog of disasters down to unfortunate circumstances and nothing else. Dinsdale, however, felt very strongly otherwise. He said, of this fraught and weird time, that having suffered such health-related calamities, he knew it was time to leave behind both Loch Ness and the distinct sense of unease he experienced whenever he visited it. "It was," Dinsdale wrote in *Loch Ness Monster*, "as though some awful influence pervaded the atmosphere. Something evil." Those are quite astonishing words for a man who, publicly, saw the Nessies as flesh-and-blood animals and nothing else.

An encounter at the witching hour

In 1970, Tim Dinsdale crossed paths with Winifred Cary. She was the psychic who Ted Holiday came to know well, and who had much to say about the Sundberg UFO sighting of 1971 and Reverend Omand's exorcism of 1973. The home she shared with her husband, Basil, overlooked Urquhart Bay, and she claimed no less than sixteen sightings of the Nessies over a period of almost sixty years. Winifred Cary was also a highly skilled dowser who said she could use her powers to seek out a Nessie. Apparently, she did exactly that. And she did far more, too: she found evidence of no less than *two* creatures in the loch. Dinsdale, very impressed by Cary's psychic skills, raced to the water's edge, jumped in his boat, and headed out to the two spots where Cary had identified monsters apparently lurking. Amazingly, Dinsdale's sonar equipment picked up something only six hundred feet from Cary's first site. More impressive, another sonar image was picked up *exactly* where Cary said a monster was present.

Again, this demonstrates that not only did Dinsdale recognize the supernatural aspects of the Loch Ness Monsters themselves, he also recognized that they could be tracked down by supernatural means—in this case, by water-divining.

Then, late one night in 1975, while negotiating the precarious hills that stand west of Urquhart Bay, en route to his boat—the appropriately named *Water Horse*—Dinsdale experienced something strange. He was shocked and terrified by the sight of a weird blue light that, very curiously, appeared to come out of the very soil itself, around 120 feet in front of him. Rather notably, the flash coincided with Dinsdale checking his watch. It was precisely midnight ... *the witching hour.* That was not good. Not good in the slightest.

Such was the intensity of the light, it lit up an entire nearby field as well as the trees that led down to the water's edge. Suddenly, there was a second flash, but this time it came from *above* the surface of the loch itself. Dinsdale took a deep breath, tried to calm himself, and took the *Water Horse* into the loch. It was all to no avail, however: the lights did not return, and no answer was ever found for what had caused them. Nevertheless, something continued to torment Dinsdale's mind. You may already have guessed what it was—yes, the almost certainly relevant matter of the curious timing. Midnight is just about the darkest and most sinister hour of all.

Loch Ness Monster authority Roland Watson notes that similar blue lights have been seen at the equally monster-infested Loch Morar, home to the legendary Morag. On top of that, Dinsdale was, on one occasion, chilled to the absolute bone by a banshee-like wailing that echoed around Loch Morar at the height of a violent 3:00 a.m. thunderstorm.

A ghostly battlefield and a tragic death in the Nessie-seeking community

Two years after quietly admitting to Ted Holiday that there appeared to be a supernatural aspect to the matter of the Loch Ness Monsters, Dinsdale yet again demonstrated his interest in matters that many assumed were far removed from the domain of the Loch Ness Monsters. In 1976, in the pages of his *Operations Newsletter*, Dinsdale wrote that not only did he hope to continue to liaise with colleagues engaged in the search for the Nessies—and also those seeking the Morags of Loch Morar—but he wished to do likewise with people doing research in the fields of alien encounters, Sasquatch, and supernatural activity.

Australian monster hunter Tony Healy met with Dinsdale, at Loch Ness, in 1979. As Roland Watson recounts, Healy later stated that Holiday did indeed have a firm belief in at least some supernatural manifestations. Indeed, Dinsdale shared with Healy the details of some of his experiences. One story in particular stands out. Incredibly, Healy revealed that on one occasion, late at night and while Dinsdale had the *Water Horse* tethered close to Fort Augustus Abbey, he, Dinsdale, heard what sounded distinctly like someone being flogged and screaming for their life. For Dinsdale, it was possibly a glimpse into the past, the sounds of someone being violently tortured at the height of what became known as the Jacobite Rebellion of 1745. This was a tumultuous battle in which "Bonnie Prince Charlie" tried—but failed—to seize the British throne for the House of Stuart.

The year 1979 also witnessed the death of Ted Holiday, who passed away from a heart attack at a prematurely young age: he was only in his late fifties. More than a few researchers who held similar views to Holiday believed that his early demise was a direct result of his attempts to confront and combat the supernatural activity that dominated Loch Ness. A tragic victim of malevolent monsters.

"They finally killed off the plesiosaur idea for him"

Four years later, in 1983, the late Eric Beckjord—a researcher who believed that just about every weird critter under the sun had supernatural origins (and, just perhaps, they do)—visited Dinsdale and learned something fascinating. According to a report in *Paranormal Underground*, Dinsdale told Beckjord how, one night while moored near Aleister Crowley's Boleskine House, he encountered all manner of supernatural entities trying to attack him and board his boat, including specters, demonic things, and ghoulish creatures. Dinsdale stressed they did him no physical harm, but as Beckjord noted, "they finally killed off the plesiosaur idea for him."

The Nessies, ghosts, and the psychic spies of the U.S. government

The mid-1970s, when Tim Dinsdale found his mind in a supernatural whirl, are noted for something else with a supernatural, Nessie-based tie-in. That was when the U.S. government—predominantly the CIA, Defense Intelligence Agency, and the U.S. Army—began to secretly fund extensive research into the phenomenon of what has become known as "remote viewing" (RV). The goal was to have skilled psychics utilize supernatural phenomena, extra-sensory perception, and out-of-body episodes to spy on—amongst others—the Russians, the Chinese, and various troublesome nations in the Middle East. The remote viewers were, then, Uncle Sam's very own paranormal 007's. In many respects they were the twentieth-century equivalents of Dr. John Dee, mixing espionage and the occult in strange and swirling fashion.

One of those who sought to understand the full scope of the remote-viewing program was the well-known conspiracy researcher and author Jim Marrs. During the course of his investigations, Marrs learned something incredible. Namely, that the "Psi Spies" had at one point focused their psychic skills on the Loch Ness Monster. In doing so, they stumbled onto something amazing, something which adds much weight to the argument that the Nessies are supernatural in nature.

Marrs said that over the course of a number of attempts to remote view the Nessies, the RV team found evidence of what appeared to be physical, living creatures—ones that left wakes and which could be photographed and tracked. They even prepared drawings that suggested the Nessies might be plesiosaurs. But there was something else, too: the ability of the creatures to vanish—as in dematerialize. The remote viewers were in a collective quandary: their work certainly supported the theory that some seriously strange creatures dwelled deep in Loch Ness, but these were creatures that seemed to have supernatural and abnormal qualities about them—which is precisely what both Ted Holiday and Tim Dinsdale finally came around to believing.

Jim Marrs notes, "Considering that reports of human ghosts date back throughout man's history, the Psi Spies seriously considered the possibility that the Loch Ness monster is nothing less than a dinosaur's ghost."

Nessie becomes a TV star

It's interesting to note that the phenomenal and worldwide coverage the Loch Ness Monsters achieved in the mid-1970s, coupled with the deep attention given to the supernatural aspects of the controversy by the likes of Ted Holiday, had an impact on the production team behind the BBC's long-running, hugely popular science-fiction series, *Dr. Who*.

From August 30 to September 20, 1975, the BBC ran "Terror of the Zygons." It was a four-part story, broadcast on Saturday evenings, which put an interesting spin on the story of the Loch Ness Monster. In much the same way that the Loch Ness creature of *The Private Life of Sherlock Holmes* was, in that movie's plot, an advanced piece of machinery—namely, a carefully camouflaged submarine—so too was the Nessie that tangled with the world's most famous fictional time traveler, Dr. Who.

The BBC and the Beast

"Terror of the Zygons" tells the story of an alien race, the Zygons of the title, whose home world was decimated and destroyed by solar flares centuries ago. As a result, they decide to create a new home for themselves. No prizes for guessing the planned location of that new home: Earth. The one solitary band of Zygons that successfully made the journey to Earth had the distinct misfortune to crash in none other than Loch Ness. And they remain there for hundreds of years, patiently planning for the day when they could finally claim Earth as their own.

To help them in their quest to seek control of the planet, the Zygons employed the use of a huge and terrifying monster known as the Skarasen. The Skarasen was an ancient beast of the deep waters which the Zygons turned into a cyborg—a half-flesh, half-machine being that did their every bidding and lived in Loch Ness; it had, of course, over time become known as the Loch Ness Monster. And that bidding included a wave of mysterious and violent attacks on oil rigs in the North Sea.

It was up to Dr. Who and his comrades—Sarah Jane Smith, Harry Sullivan, and Brigadier Lethbridge-Stewart—to defeat the deadly Zygons. Fortunately, Dr. Who finally saved the day, as he always does. Although not before the Skarasen-Nessie wreaked havoc in and around London's River Thames and the Zygons did their very best to take hold of the planet.

There can be little doubt that the writing team behind the story had some knowledge of the lore and legend of Nessie. After all, the creature is presented as not just an unknown animal; far from it, in fact. In addition, the story does not shy away from the UFO-themed connections to Loch Ness. And let's not overlook something else of great importance: the masters and manipulators of the Loch Ness Monster, the Zygons, are diabolical shapeshifters who can take on the form of any human being they choose—not unlike the murderous kelpies and water-horses of centuries long past that haunted Loch Ness and terrified the local folk. Although strictly fiction, "Terror of the Zygons" provided an intriguing and thought-provoking scenario to explain the mystery of the Loch Ness Monster.

Also thought-provoking and intriguing was a startling discovery made at Loch Ness in 1976; a discovery no one could ever have anticipated, which occurred slightly less than a year after "Terror of the Zygons" was broadcast. As will now be demonstrated ...

21

Stonehenge to Loch Ness

One of the most confounding things about cryptids is their curious connection to ancient stone circles, sites of archaeological significance, and historical burial mounds. The United Kingdom's most famous stone circle, Stonehenge, is situated on the vast and sprawling Salisbury Plain, which is located in the green and hilly county of Wiltshire. Notably, sightings of strange creatures near this approximately five-thousand-year-old Neolithic stone structure are far from uncommon. As just one example among many, George Price, a former member of the British Army, had a sighting of a huge, orangutan-like animal on Salisbury Plain in 2002, an encounter he shared with Merrily Harpur, a researcher of large, anomalous black cats in the UK.

The English county of Kent is home to a small village called Blue Bell Hill, which happens to be the site of a Neolithic-era formation of stones called Kit's Coty House (the Neolithic period having begun prior to 10,000 BC and come to an end around 2,000 BC). Kit's Coty House is a structure that may have doubled as a site for human sacrifice and a memorial to ancient fallen warriors of renown. It's notable that numerous sightings have been made at Kit's Coty House—usually late at night, and often when the moon is full and a cold wind howls—of semi-spectral, primitive-looking people, dressed in rags and animal skins, lurking amongst the old, long-abandoned stones.

England's Peak District is the site of a millennia-old stone circle known locally as the Nine Ladies. What can only be described as a hulking British Bigfoot was seen in the area in 1991. The Bronze Age Rollright Stones of Oxfordshire are haunted by a large, shaggy beast that is a strange and savage combination of ape and wolf. Lustleigh Cleave is an earthworks built in Neolithic times and located on Dartmoor, Devon, where Sir Arthur Conan Doyle set his classic Sherlock Holmes novel *The Hound of the Baskervilles*. The deadly dog of Doyle's acclaimed story was fictional. The hairy "cave men" that, for centuries, have been seen roaming around Lustleigh Cleave on starlit winter nights are most assuredly not.

Zoomorphic spirit guardians

So, what's going on? Why are monsters and strange creatures so inextricably linked to old stone circles and formations? A notable theory comes from Linda Godfrey, a resident of Wisconsin and someone who has extensively investigated, and written about, bizarre animals in her home state as well as across the entirety of the United States. In the same way that unidentified creatures are seen in the direct vicinities of stone circles in the UK, Linda has noted that such is also the case in the United States, where similar "things" are encountered near old Native American mounds—particularly, beasts that sound chillingly like real-life werewolves. Linda says, "I can tell you that Native Americans from various locations have indicated to me that these things absolutely exist, as do zoomorphic [animal-shaped] spirit guardians made to watch over sacred grounds."

This is a fascinating scenario: ancient man may very well have tapped into a hard-to-define realm of the supernatural and duly called forth fantastic beasts to act, in essence, as paranormal guard dogs of revered sites of a mystical nature. All of which brings us to the matter of the monsters of Loch Ness. It's a little-known fact that the loch itself has its very own, and very mysterious, stone structures. Should we simply chalk this up to coincidence? Based on what you are now about to read, my answer to that question can only be a decisive "No."

"A mother lode of stone circles— big ones and little ones"

The summer of 1976 was noted for being one of the hottest on record in the UK, something that anyone of a certain age, who lived through it, can attest to. By June, the temperature was already up to the mid-80s Fahrenheit. On July 3, it peaked at a pulverizing 96.6 Fahrenheit. That scalding period was noted for something else, too: an American named Marty Klein was at Loch Ness as part of an expedition to find evidence of the existence of its famous creatures. It was an ambitious quest, organized and sponsored by the Academy of Applied Science and the *New York Times* and headed by long-time Nessie-seeker Dr. Robert H. Rines. It was also a project that saw the AAS team capture some intriguing sonar imagery, including one—dubbed the "average plesiosaur"—that seemed to show nothing less than a long-necked carcass in the deep waters off Fort Augustus, Loch Ness. But there was something else that Klein and his comrades found—something that was as amazing as it was surely unanticipated.

While using side-scan sonar technology in the waters near the village of Lochend, on the northeastern end of the loch, the team stumbled on something hitherto unknown: two curious formations, one in water of a depth of barely thirty feet, and another at a depth of around seventy feet. According to science writer Dennis Meredith, they had found "a mother lode of stone circles—big ones and little ones; single circles and circles intertwined with others; circles laid out in a straight line and circles in no particular order."

Given that Marty Klein was *the* key figure in the discovery of the stones, they became known—almost inevitably—as Kleinhenge I and Kleinhenge II. In terms of size, the circles ranged from fifteen to one hundred and fifty feet in diameter. And, to varying degrees, they overlapped.

Not everyone was sure that the henges had Neolithic origins, which was something quickly suggested by the AAS when the formations were found. One J. D. Mills, of the Surrey, England-based Underwater Instrumentation, offered the theory that the stones were nothing stranger than material dredged from the nearby River Ness when the building of the Caledonian Canal was underway early in the nineteenth century. But is this really all there was to the Kleinhenges? Others have suggested that such a down-to-earth explanation is very wide of the mark.

Nessie and Neolithic mysteries

When the story of the stone circles of Loch Ness got out, Klein and a colleague, Charles Finkelstein, told the *Chicago Tribune's* John Noble Wilford that while a great deal of further research was required, it was their initial conclusion that the formations were fashioned by human hand and that they quite possibly dated back thousands of years, to a time when the waters of the loch were at much lower levels than today. Then, in 2005, Robert Rines commented on *yet more* curious formations of stones found in the deep waters of the loch; Loch Ness Monster authority Roland Watson has contemplated—but is admittedly not persuaded by—the idea that the sunken stones referenced by Rines in 2005 could likewise be a by-product of the completion of the Caledonian Canal in 1822 or of the widening of the A82 road back in the 1930s. And the controversy does not end there.

The curious case of the Clava Cairns

There is an undeniable similarity between Kleinhenge I and II and what are known as the Balnuaran of Clava, or the Clava Cairns. Like the previously mentioned Kit's Coty House and Lustleigh Cleave, the Balnuaran of Clava date back to the Neolithic era, probably around 2,000 BC. In essence they are a trio of burial chambers, found above Scotland's River Nairn amid enchanting woodland, and are positioned in north-to-east and south-to-west directions. The passages leading to the chambers were created in a fashion that deliberately aligned them to the setting of the midwinter sun. Clearly, then, the construction process was a matter of deep importance and significance to their creators.

Just like the Kleinhenges, the Clava Cairns are comprised of stones, pebbles, and even boulders heaped together in circular, raised formations. Their purpose: to act as sacred burial chambers for the elite figures of the tribe in question; a theory bolstered by the fact that when the tombs were excavated in both the 1800s and the 1950s, the cremated remains of a number of select people were found within.

A flying monster enters the mix

Very interestingly, the Clava Cairns are located off the B9006 road and east of Inverness, only a short drive from Loch Ness. Of equal note, the River Nairn—on which the cairns stand—flows into the Moray Firth, as does the River Ness, the latter having been the site of a number of creature encounters, including the now-legendary and famous 565 AD account of St. Columba.

Adding even more monster-based bizarreness to the story, the River Nairn flows by the site of a historic April 16, 1746, confrontation. Its name: the Battle of Culloden. Scottish lore tells of how, on the night before the violent battle began, a huge, monstrous, bird-like beast was seen hovering and flying above the battlefield. Known as the Skree, this Mothman-style creature had eyes that blazed red, and large and membranous wings like those of a hideous, devilish bat. The creature was seen as a decidedly ill-omen, a precursor to the death and tragedy that loomed on the horizon for the opposing forces of Bonnie Prince Charlie and George II. It was a battle that brought to an end what was known as the Jacobite Rising.

So what we have here, within the waters of Loch Ness and at the Clava Cairns—on the nearby River Nairn—are curious stone structures that are eerily similar. Loch Ness is home to one of the world's most legendary cryptids. The nearby River Nairn is linked to sightings of a flying, fiery-eyed monster. And the Clava Cairns were created to house the cremated remains of tribal chieftains. All of this brings us back to Linda Godfrey's comments in relation to Native American lore. Namely, that animal-shaped spirit guardians—summoned up via magical rite in the distant past—possibly watch over and protect sacred and significant sites. Just perhaps, then, at least some of the Nessies are similar spirit guardians. They may still faithfully watch over the now-sunken old stone circles of Loch Ness—ones that were constructed millennia ago by a tribe of people now utterly forgotten and lost to the fog of time. Perhaps that's why, as kelpies, the creatures demonstrated such hostility to anyone who, probably unknowingly, got too close to those ancient structures.

From this idea of spirit guardians, we now need to address the relationship between the Nessies and the dead: a restless specter.

—— 22 ——
A Military Ghost and the Monsters

The strange and near-enigmatic Stonehenge-like structures were not the only things discovered in Loch Ness by Marty Klein's team in 1976. They also stumbled upon the remains of a Second World War–era aircraft. It was a Vickers Wellington Bomber, the brainchild of one Barnes Wallis, who created a revolutionary "bouncing bomb" during the hostilities with the Nazis that was designed to destroy German dams. The Dam-Busters, as the team that dropped the bombs was known, succeeded beyond their wildest dreams, leaving a significant scar on Hitler's war machine. When Klein's group stumbled on the remains of the bomber, a great deal of interest was exhibited by military historians and aviation enthusiasts. The race for its recovery was well and truly on—although for years afterwards, the aircraft remained where it had already sat for more than thirty years; that is to say, approximately 230 feet beneath the surface of the loch.

It wasn't just Klein's people that were fascinated by the discovery. So was Heriot-Watt University's Underwater Technology Unit. The results of the investigations by both groups, along with help provided by the British Royal Navy, conclusively identified the aircraft as a Wellington. They even managed to identify its serial number: N2980. There was nothing particularly mysterious about N2980: as far back as late 1939, it had taken part in no less than fourteen bombing missions over Germany before being transferred to Lossiemouth, where it was then used to train newly drafted aircrews. Official records on the crash were quickly accessed and told a memorable story.

Tragedy at Loch Ness

Military records showed that the aircraft ditched into Loch Ness on December 31, 1940—New Year's Eve—after experiencing problems with one of the engines during a turbulent snowstorm high above the domain of monsters. It was when the crew was over the Monadhliath Mountains—which are to the southeast of Loch Ness—that problems began. They were problems that led squadron leader Nigel Marwood-Elton to give a hasty order to jump ship, so to speak; four crew members quickly parachuted out of the plane. Tragically, one of them, the twenty-year-old rear gunner, Sergeant John Stanley Fensome, was killed when his parachute catastrophically wrapped itself around one of the wings of the doomed plane.

While the crew was racing to exit the aircraft, Marwood-Elton and the co-pilot, named Slater, stayed onboard, struggling to control the aircraft as the dusky skies threatened to give way to darkness. With the snow hammering down and a powerful wind blowing, they maneuvered the plane closer and closer to the loch and, incredibly, actually managed to land it on the surface of the water, ditching near Urquhart Castle. With water already flooding into the aircraft from all corners, they scrambled for an onboard dinghy. The two then clambered out of the plane and onto the starboard wing, where they inflated the dinghy and used it to row to shore as the aircraft was swallowed up by the waves, practically intact. As they reached land, the two men managed to flag down an astonished truck driver, who quickly drove them to Inverness—no doubt for a couple of wee and hearty drams to help steady their nerves.

It wasn't until September 1985, amid more than a few hazards and hiccups, that the bulk of the aircraft was finally raised from the water, with the recovery of numerous scattered fragments continuing into 1986. Incredibly, and almost unbelievably, the taillights of the plane were still in good working order. The well-preserved remains of N2980 can now be seen on display at the Brooklands Museum in Surrey, England.

Now we come to the strangest parts of the story—those that are focused on nothing less than the world of the paranormal, the domain of the afterlife, and those mysterious creatures that have, for so long, haunted Loch Ness.

"Confronted by a ghost"

As noted above, the Vickers Wellington N2980 was found in 1976 by Marty Klein's team and was conclusively identified in 1979. It was in 1978, however, that the Underwater Technology Group secured clear images of the aircraft, using high-tech cameras designed for use in deep waters. It may not be a coincidence that 1978 was also the year in which sightings began at Loch Ness of a spectral figure wearing a Second World War–era British Royal Air Force uniform. Was this the restless spirit of the one crew member, Sergeant John Stanley Fensome, who lost his life on the final flight of N2980? Did the filming of the aircraft disturb his supernatural slumber? Just perhaps, that's precisely what happened.

As one example of more than a few, there is the story of a man named Peter Smithson, who told ghost investigator Bruce Barrymore

Halpenny of his encounter with the ghostly airman in 1978. Smithson said it was early one morning, just as dawn was breaking, when he saw someone coming towards him—from the depths of Loch Ness. Smithson's first reaction—and a quite natural reaction—was to assume there had been some kind of accident.

It is easy to understand why Smithson assumed this, as the man before him was dressed in military clothing and was dragging behind him a parachute. But what baffled Smithson was the fact that the uniform the man was wearing was clearly out of date. It was far from modern-looking and far more befitted the 1940s, when the world was engaged in trying to defeat the hordes of Adolf Hitler. Smithson shouted to the man to see if he was okay. The response he got was an eerie one: the man turned slightly and pointed towards the waters of Loch Ness. Smithson said that the man then suddenly dematerialized, leaving him with a "funny feeling" and a suspicion that what he had seen was "a ghost airman." He commented, "What a damn fool I felt, confronted by a ghost, my camera around my neck, yet I never had an inkling to take a photo."

A Nessie checks out the Wellington

The weirdness just gets better: aircraft enthusiast and writer Joseph W. Zarzynski was approached by a man named Murdo Urquhart, who said that on September 15, 1985—when the operation to recover N2980 was in full swing—he saw nothing less than a Nessie moving across the surface of the loch, practically on top of the site where the aircraft sank. Perhaps of relevance, on the very same day that Urquhart encountered the creature, a fishing net that was sitting next to the wreck became mysteriously caught up in ... something.

So, what we have here is the crash of a wartime bomber, one that, in 1978, led to the out-of-the-blue appearance of a spectral airman. An airman whose watery grave had possibly been disturbed for the very first time since New Year's Eve, 1940. Then we have the appearance of a mysterious creature at the very same haunted location in 1985. And people still believe that the Loch Ness monsters are nothing but giant eels, oversized salamanders, or relic populations of plesiosaurs?

Yes, people do continue to hold that belief. What happened in May 1977, however, may well make more than a few reassess those beliefs.

23

A Wizard of the Waters

Roughly twelve months after the discovery of the Kleinhenges, one of the most controversial but fascinating figures in the saga of the Loch Ness Monster made his way to that legendary body of water that has captivated so many for so long. His name was, and indeed still is, Anthony "Doc" Shiels. He is a wizard, surrealist, conjurer, and someone who may very well have mastered the art of performing what one might call *real* magic. Doc has performed rites and rituals that may have opened doorways to other realms of existence, allowing monstrous entities to intrude upon, and rampage around, our own world.

These beings include the Owlman—a feathered, nightmarish flying humanoid that terrorized the good folk of Mawnan, England—and Morgawr, a long-necked, supernatural sea serpent seen off the coast of England on numerous occasions. Sightings of both began in the summer of 1976. This just happened to be the exact same time in which Kleinhenge I and II were being excitedly studied at Loch Ness.

Born in 1938, Shiels is part "Wizard of the Western World," part trickster, part stage magician and playwright. He's someone whose approach to monster hunting hardly endears him to the field of regular cryptozoology ("regular cryptozoology," of course, perhaps being the ultimate oxymoron!). It's not surprising, then, that this has led more than a few observers to view Shiels's words, findings, conclusions, and photographs (of Nessie, no less) to be less than sound. Too bad for them. Those who hold such views have utterly failed to understand and appreciate what it means to be Doc Shiels. His is a world filled with a deep understanding of the genuine nature and power of magic (both the chaos and ritualistic kind), of the secrets of invocation and manifestation, of the "game of the name" that Ted Holiday experienced in relation to Dr. John Dee, of strange realms just beyond—and that occasionally interact with—our own, and of that aforementioned trickster-like phenomenon.

Doc's is also a domain where, when we dare to imagine the fantastic, when we decide to seek it out, and when we finally accept its reality (not forgetting that it can be as manipulative and malignant as it can be illuminating and playful), we perhaps provide it with some form of quasi-existence in our very own world. In short, perhaps we give birth to monsters by the mere means of thinking about them and duly demanding they appear for us. All of which brings us to the matter of the Loch Ness Monster and the input of this master magician.

Summoning the serpents of the deep

The climax to the story concerning how Doc Shiels became part and parcel of the Loch Ness legend came on the afternoon of May 21, 1977. But it's the months preceding that momentous date that we have to first focus our attention upon. It was during this period that Shiels hooked up with a collection of like-minded psychics who called themselves the PSI: the Psychic Seven International. It was an ambitious project, one in which Shiels and a team of "skyclad" (that's to say, utterly butt-naked) witches performed complex rites, of a supernatural nature, on the shores of a variety of lakes in Ireland and Scotland that had monster traditions and legends attached to them. Shiels said that the goal of the PSI was to invoke the presence of supernatural sea serpents and lake monsters across the planet.

Very appropriately for such a project, the first attempt, which lasted for three whole days, commenced on January 31. It marked the date of the Pagan festival of Imbolc—which is one of the four key festivals of the Irish calendar, celebrated as winter gives way to spring. Originally dedicated to the Pagan goddess Brigid, in the early years of Christianity in the British Isles the festival was changed to St. Brigid's Day, and the legends of Brigid were re-worked into the story of the Christian saint of the same name. The alternate name of the festival, in Scotland, is La Fheill Brighde.

As history has shown, the rites performed by the members of PSI may very well have succeeded worldwide. Lake monsters and sea serpents were soon spotted in Lake Kok-kol in eastern Kazakhstan; in Scotland's Loch Morar; and even in the heart of the San Francisco Bay. On top of that, and of even greater significance, on January 31 there were no less than three separate sightings of a Nessie—by Pat Scott-Innes, a Mr. and Mrs. Alex McLeod, and a Mr. Fleming and his young daughter, Helen. Four months later, Shiels saw the fruits of his magical labors for himself—and in undeniable, spectacular fashion.

The wizard captures the monster—on film

In May 1977, Shiels and his wife, Chris, took a train from their Truro, Cornwall, England home to the heart of mysterious, ancient Scotland. It was a trip destined to have an amazing and controversy-filled outcome. Matters all began early on the morning of Saturday, May 21. The Shiels, along with two friends, Richard and Lynn Smith of Carharrack, and a couple from the English town of Bolton, were standing and chatting on the car park of the hotel in which they were all staying: the Inchnacardoch Lodge, which overlooks Loch Ness's Inchnacardoch Bay. Suddenly, Chris noticed something amazing: three significantly sized humps that snaked through the waters of Loch Ness in the direction of Fort Augustus. Whether one large creature or three entirely separate and smaller ones, it was impossible to tell, but the important thing was that *something* was there, for all six to see and marvel upon.

Disastrously, not a single one of them had a camera at hand—which was hardly a surprise, since their only reason for standing outside was to await the opening of the breakfast area. Shiels considered making a dash for their hotel-room, but was thwarted from doing so when the three humps slipped beneath the waves and the beast, or beasts, was gone. It was something that mirrored the lessons learned by Ted Holiday: the Nessies and cameras are not always the best of friends. Shiels learned a cautionary lesson himself: he vowed never again to be camera-free while hanging out at Loch Ness. It was a very wise decision, as the events of only a few hours later spectacularly served to demonstrate.

After partaking of a few pints of Guinness and a couple of single malts in the hotel bar, Doc and Chris walked towards Urquhart Castle from the Lewiston road. As they did so, the pair noticed a number of curious wakes in the water, something which was a mild precursor to what was very quickly to follow.

A media sensation and a monster

Around 4:00 p.m., Doc decided to climb the castle's old Grant Tower and scan the expansive waters it overlooked. To his amazement, in just mere moments and as if right on cue, what appeared to be a very small head broke the surface of the loch. It was followed by a long, serpent-like neck. The creature was clearly of a significant size, since the portion of the neck that could be seen was protruding out of the water to a height of at least four to five feet—never mind how much more was still *underneath* the water. Interestingly, Shiels had a sudden feeling that the creature had actually readied itself to be photographed by him. He quickly snapped a couple of shots, which displayed the animal's green-brown neck and its pale, somewhat yellowish front. The head was absurdly small and the mouth continually agape. In moments, it sank beneath the surface of the loch.

Doc was *beyond* delighted, as was Chris, when he quickly and excitedly told her of what he had just seen and photographed. Despite the pair diligently checking out the loch for the next few days, nothing else of a meaningful nature occurred. It was now time to head back home to Cornwall and get the photographs developed—as in quick-fire time. The reel of film was handed over to a local journalist and friend, David Clarke, who in turn gave it to Newquay Color Services, a company that did most of the developing for a local magazine Clarke worked on, *Cornish Life*. To the delight of David and Doc, the images looked near-perfect: Shiels had caught the beast in just about the best pose possible. Some suggested the best pose was just too good to be true, which is hardly surprising given Doc's reputation as a skilled magician and wizard. There are, however, strong reasons why we should *not* consider the photos to be examples of nothing stranger than expert fakery.

Doc quickly contacted another local journalist and friend, Mike Truscott, who immediately put a call in to the Glasgow, Scotland, *Daily Record* newspaper. The news desk expressed major interest in Doc's pictures. The photo editor at the *Daily Record*, Martin Gilfeather, requested that Doc send—via train, for speed—both processed pictures, for his team to see and study. It was wise of Doc, as it turned out, that he chose to only send only one. To his credit,

Gilfeather asked for the rest of the film to be sent as well, so that he could confirm Doc and Chris really had been in Scotland, and specifically at the loch.

Gilfeather's study of the negatives demonstrated that the photos of the Nessie were taken exactly where Doc had claimed: at Loch Ness. Indeed, as the roll of negative showed, the two images were sandwiched right in between a variety of other shots of Loch Ness, Urqhuart Castle, and the Inchnacardoch Lodge Hotel. Gilfeather even phoned the hotel to get confirmation that the Shiels had stayed there. The owner confirmed they did, and on the very days in question. Impressed by all of this validation, it wasn't long before the *Daily Record* published the story—as did the *Daily Mirror*, one of the nation's biggest-selling newspapers. At this point things got very strange and dark.

"Tim Dinsdale had warned me about this kind of thing"

As Shiels himself noted, "The newspaper promised to send all my pictures back at once, but it was almost two nail-biting weeks before I received the monster slide. My 'holiday snaps' had been 'temporarily displaced.' I haven't seen them since. Tim Dinsdale had warned me about this kind of thing."

Things got even stranger: David Blenchley, a Falmouth-based photographer, had mailed a copy of one of the priceless images to a man named Max Maven—a psychic, magician, American member of the Psychic Seven International team, and someone who, in later years, worked with the acclaimed stage magicians Penn and Teller. Somewhere between Falmouth, England, and Boston, Massachusetts, the image vanished from what was a well-sealed and protected package. It was never seen again. Another attempt to share the image failed miserably when a glass slide prepared by

Cornwall journalist Frank Durham was accidentally broken and shattered into pieces. Shiels, acutely aware of the power of real magic, viewed all of this as a kind of growing supernatural menace. It wasn't the end of the story, however. There was far worse to come.

Dr. David Hoy, who was part of the PSI team, suffered a heart attack; Major Leslie May, also of the team, was stricken with ill-health; several of the members investigating the sightings at Lake Kok-kol vanished without a trace; Doc had a son injured in a motorbike accident; one of his daughters was thrown by a horse; another daughter was hit by mysterious stomach pains; the family's pair of pet cats died; and—rather bizarrely—Doc accidentally set his beard on fire, with no lasting effects, fortunately.

Not surprisingly, Shiels knew when it was time to back off. And the time was now. Doc knew he had been pushing his luck throughout the entire exercise, but it was clear he had pushed that luck way too far. The backlash had reached breaking point, a dark development which, on July 7, 1977, led Shiels to sever all ties with the rest of the people attached to the experiments to raise monsters.

An affidavit and expert commentary

On November 14, 1977, Shiels prepared and signed an affidavit that, in part, stated he was of a firm opinion that the two images he secured did indeed show a Nessie in Loch Ness—utterly genuine Nessies and not the work of photo manipulation or hoaxing. Tim Dinsdale quickly got in the act. He sent the original first image— shared with him by Shiels—to a Dr. Vernon Harrison, who, until 1976, had held the prestigious position of President of the Royal Photographic Society. Dr. Harrison, in his typewritten reply to Dinsdale, came straight to the point: "I find the transparency to be quite normal and there is no evidence of double exposure, super-imposition of images or handwork with bleach or dye." He added that the water appeared disturbed around the base of the neck, and that this had created distortions which were precisely what one would expect to see in an image that showed a partly submerged animal. Harrison did try to come up with rational explanations for all of his observations, such as the monster actually being a large-scale model ingeniously moved and manipulated by a diver below the surface of the loch, or the image being a photograph of a well-executed oil-painting. He admitted, though, that both theories were, at the very best, hardly likely.

Quite so. And to have these statements come from such a prestigious source as Dr. Harrison proved to be a major victory for Shiels as he sought to have his photos of the creatures of the loch—as well as his theory that he had psychically summoned the Nessie in question—vindicated.

And this was not to be Shiels's last run-in with the Loch Ness monsters, as we shall now see.

24

Doc Shiels Returns

In 1981, Doc Shiels found himself caught up in yet another aspect of the Loch Ness Monster saga—a saga that once again reinforced the paranormal origins of the beast. In the same way that, in 1977, Shiels had attempted, and apparently succeeded, in summoning up a creature of the loch, he attempted to do likewise at a number of Irish lakes some four years later. One of those lakes was Lough Leane, a nineteen-square-kilometer body of water situated near Killarney. Shiels had a very good reason for focusing on this particular lake. It is said to be the final resting place of a collection of priceless treasure that belonged to a legendary warrior of old named O'Donoghue. Not only that, the treasure is said to be fiercely guarded by a great three-headed worm. So, with this in mind, Doc attempted to call forth the wormy monster of Killarney.

On this occasion, Shiels was far less successful than he had been at Loch Ness: the monster flatly refused to manifest. There was, however, one very interesting, and strange, development. At the height of Shiels's attempts to raise water monsters in Ireland, he encountered a young man named Patrick O'Talbot Kelly, a resident of County Mayo. By Shiels's own admission, Kelly was an unusual character, one who seemed to know far more about the Shiels family than Doc preferred him to know. So when Kelly offered to help Doc invoke monstrous serpents, Doc politely declined. Kelly shrugged his shoulders and went on his way and was not seen again—at least, not for another four years. In 1985, however, Kelly resurfaced. Not from the depths of Lough Leane, though, it should be stressed!

Aleister Crowley re-enters the Nessie saga

During the four years that had passed by, Kelly moved to live in the United States and, while there, made the acquaintance of a friend of Doc named Masklyn—who, just like Doc, was also a skilled magician. Masklyn wasted no time in letting Doc know what was going down. As Doc listened, it became quickly clear that Patrick Kelly was far more than just someone with a passion for monster hunting. Kelly asserted to Masklyn that he could claim a lineage that went back to Elizabethan times and to the previously referred-to powerful occultist Edward Kelly. Remember, Aleister Crowley asserted he was the reincarnation of Edward Kelly.

When, in 1981, Doc Shiels attempted to raise monsters at Ireland's Lough Leane, he had failed to see anything unusual. But *someone* saw something strange, and that someone was Patrick Kelly. He claimed to have encountered, and photographed, a humped, long-necked monster in the lough. He duly sent the photo to Shiels as proof. The beast, Shiels noted, closely resembled a sea serpent seen off the coast of Cornwall, England in the scalding hot summer of 1976. Its name, as we have already seen, was Morgawr. And the high-strangeness doesn't end there.

According to what Patrick Kelly told magician Masklyn, Kelly's father, Laurence, was a close acquaintance of none other than Aleister Crowley. Who, as we have seen, played far more than a passing role in the saga of the monsters of Loch Ness. The pair had apparently met in Paris, France, in 1933—intriguingly, the very year in which the story of the Loch Ness Monster erupted in sensational, worldwide fashion. Crowley had told Laurence Kelly that he was deeply interested in the developments at Loch Ness. Crowley also emphasized to Laurence how he had called forth supernatural entities from the depths of the loch years earlier. It was a revelation which prompted Laurence to take his son, Patrick, to the loch in 1969—the very year that a curious, wormy tapestry was found near Boleskine House and which plunged Ted Holiday into a state of anxiety.

Dragon expert Richard Freeman, in view of all this, has asked a valid question: "Could Patrick Kelly and his father have been performing some kind of ritual at Loch Ness?" Just perhaps, that's *exactly* what happened. From the long-gone days of Aleister Crowley to Patrick Kelly in both 1969 and the 1980s, the lure of Loch Ness's world of the supernatural may have been impossible to resist.

The legends of Lough Leane

Finally, as to this story, it's notable that Lough Leane, which played a central role in this entire affair, has a curious legend attached to it. Centuries-old lore tells of a powerful Irish warrior named Oison, of the Fianna clan, who, while hunting in the area of the lake, took a break at its shores. As he did so, a beautiful woman suddenly appeared amid the early morning, floating across the water in the direction of Fianna. Her name: Niamh Cinn Lir—or Niamh of the Golden Hair. She invited entranced Oison to come with her to her home, a land called Tir na N'ogm, which translates as "the land of the young." As the name suggests, it was a magical realm where life was everlasting and aging was nonexistent. Oison agreed to go and the two quickly fell in love. After three years, however, Oison wished to pay his old world a visit.

Niamh warned Oison not to return, but when she realized how adamant he was, she said, "Take my magical horse, but never get off the horse, or you will never be able to return to Tir na Nog." Oison nodded and agreed. On returning, Oison was shocked to see that while only three years had passed in the land of the young, *three hundred* years had passed in the world above. As for his friends and family, they were all dead; long dead. And the Fianna warriors were no more. Realizing that the world he knew no longer existed, Oison decided to return to his beloved Niamh. As he motioned the horse to turn around, however, Oison fell to the ground, the stirrup having broken. As he hit the earth, Oison suddenly began to age, and death quickly followed. In moments, there was nothing but bones and a few strands of clothing. After that, just dust. Oison was gone and Niamh was heartbroken.

Of course, this is just a legend of the type that can be found all across the ancient Celtic lands of Ireland and Scotland. It should be noted, however, that the description of Niamh being a magical being who rose from the waters, and who rode a supernatural horse, gives rise to kelpie-style imagery. The kelpie, recall, was a creature that could shapeshift from a horse to a beautiful maiden and back again. This suggests that the story of Oison and Niamh may have been based on ancient sightings of kelpies in Lough Leane—and of the exact type that Patrick Kelly photographed in 1981.

We will return to Doc Shiels in due course; in the meantime, however, we move forward a few years, specifically to the late 1980s and then the early 1990s. These are periods noted for two quests to find the Nessies, but which are just about as different as it is possible to get.

— **25** —
Deep-Scanning and Calling Forth a Monster

Operation Deepscan was a highly ambitious October 1987 effort to seek out the Nessies with sonar, and it just may have had some degree of success. No less than two dozen boats were utilized to scan the depths of Loch Ness with echo-sounding equipment. Some of the presumed anomalies recorded were actually nothing stranger than tree stumps. Others may have been a seal or two which wandered into the loch. Nevertheless, there was a moment of excitement when something large and unidentified was tracked near Urquhart Bay, roughly 600 feet below the surface. It prompted Darrell Lowrance of Lowrance Electronics—whose echo-sounding equipment was used in Operation Deepscan—to say, "There's something here that we don't understand; and there's something here that's larger than a fish, maybe some species that hasn't been detected before. I don't know."

An alternative approach to monster hunting

Today, Jonathan Downes is the director of the Center for Fortean Zoology, one of the very few organizations in the world that investigates unknown animals such as the Loch Ness Monster, the

Abominable Snowman, and Mothman on a full-time basis. Back in 1992, however, Downes was spending his time working as a psychiatric nurse, as a trader in rare vinyl records, and in PR for a famous British rocker of the 1970s, Steve Harley, who was a vocalist with the band Cockney Rebel. It was while Downes was busy selling albums and singles at a record-collecting fair in the English town of Brentwood that he crossed paths with a man—Spike— who told Downes something remarkable. Clad all in black, elegantly wasted, and pale as a vampire, Spike was what is known as a chaos magician. Andrieh Vitimus, author of *Hands-On Chaos Magic*, describes this as "an attitude, a philosophy that promotes experimentation, play, and creativity while discarding dogmatic rules."

Jon Downes related what happened when he invited the Gothlike Spike to take a seat at the record fair. He recounts in *Monster Hunter* that "[Spike] told me how—together with his friends—he had carried out experiments to raise demonic entities. He … had been involved in a series of rituals designed to invoke the Babylonian snake goddess, Tiamat, on the shores of Loch Ness. He claimed that as a result of his magical incantations, he had seen a head and neck of the Loch Ness Monster looming at him out of the misty lake." Tiamat, remember, became part and parcel of Ted Holiday's theories about that certain curious tapestry found near Boleskine House in 1969.

Not long after speaking with Spike, Jon Downes had the opportunity to visit Loch Ness, choosing to go where Spike had gone some years earlier: in search of a monster.

"I had brought a bottle of wine with me to steady my nerves"

Jon Downes related that as he and his ex-wife, Alison, and two friends—Kim and Paul—drove alongside Boleskine House, he got a distinct chill, realizing that he was deep in the black heart of Aleister Crowley territory. After checking out the exterior of the old house and taking a few photos, the four headed off to find a suitable place to camp for the night—which they did, on Loch Ness's north side.

After a night out, with fine wine and equally fine dining, and much talk in a local pub of the Loch Ness Monster variety, Downes decided to take the plunge, as it were. Dawn had barely arrived on the scene when he quietly and stealthily crawled out of his sleeping bag—so as not to disturb the others or alert them to what he was about to do. He dug into his rucksack, pulled out a tape recorder, and took it and his briefcase on a brief walk down to the loch's edge. As he crept past the tent in which Kim and Paul were sleeping, Downes could hear the distinct sounds of snoring. That was a very good sign; no one knew what he was up to.

There was an issue involved in using chaos magic to invoke a Nessie that Downes found, admittedly, a little controversial: "All the celebrants in an invocation to Tiamat had to be naked. Furthermore, an offering of 'the male essence' had to be made in supplication." This was, to say the least, a highly alternative way of catching sight of a Nessie. Cameras and sonar equipment had worked on occasion. Downes, however, was about to enter what was, for him at least, uncharted territory. To say that his nerves were jerky would be an understatement. Indeed, Downes notes that "I had brought a bottle of wine with me to steady my nerves and although it was only just after six in the morning, I took a hearty swig."

Fortunately, or unfortunately, the sounds of voices from other campers interrupted Downes's plans. The moment—and the task in hand—had come and gone. Or, rather, it hadn't come—for Downes, anyway. The invocation-that-never-was may not have reached its—ahem—climax, but the affair is notable for one specific reason. Jon Downes is one of the United Kingdom's leading monster hunters, and even *he* was compelled to go after Nessie according to the teachings of magic—in this case, chaos magic. More and more, and as time advances, the futile attempts to find and identify Nessie via sonar and photography are giving way to far more esoteric means. And this was not the only occasion in the 1990s on which Jon Downes sought to cross paths with supernatural serpents of the deep.

Summoning Morgawr the sea monster

In the summer of 1998, Jon Downes—along with Richard Freeman, who was the zoological director of the Center for Fortean Zoology (and a former head keeper at England's Twycross Zoo), and various and sundry members of the CFZ—sought to raise from the seas off the coast of Devon, England, the supernatural form of Morgawr. This was the clearly paranormal long-necked sea serpent that Doc Shiels had pursued back in 1976, one year before he photographed a Nessie. The CFZ had received a request, just a week earlier, from a local television company making a documentary on sea serpents. And, of course, Downes and his crew were pleased to oblige. On the morning in question, Freeman took to the shore and stood with his legs spread wide, impressive in a long black robe and brandishing a fierce-looking sword toward the sea. He chanted an ancient invocation in a mixture of Gaelic and old English in an attempt to summon the ancient sea beast from its lair.

This was no casual, last-minute action on the part of Freeman, who as well as being a zoologist is a fully-fledged ritual magician. He had prepared well in advance. Four large candles were positioned on the sand—which amazingly stayed alight despite the rain and a powerful wind. The candles were not merely there for effect, however. A red-colored candle represented fire. A green one, the Earth. The air was portrayed in the form of a yellow candle. And the sea by a blue one.

With the time, the setting, and the atmosphere all in alignment, Freeman tossed a bunch of elderberries into the water, essentially as a gift to Morgawr. As Downes recalls, the magician then screamed at the top of his lungs: "Come ye out Morgawr; come ye out ancient sea dragon; come ye out great old one!"

The entire CFZ team, as well as the TV crew, turned slowly and apprehensively away from Freeman—whose face had briefly become like that of someone deep in the throes of demonic possession—towards the harsh, pounding waves. Unfortunately, Morgawr failed to put in an appearance that day. Yet like Downes's experience at Loch Ness in 1992, this particular episode demonstrates that for seekers of monsters of the deep waters, technology is increasingly giving way to the occult traditions of the days of old. Today, it's far less about photographing and recording the Loch Ness Monsters and their ilk and far more about supernaturally invoking them.

For some, that may involve making sacrifices to the monster. And so the story of Nessie gets even stranger. Right now.

26

Human Sacrifice in the Twentieth Century

As we have seen, back in the late 1960s Ted Holiday came to believe there existed somewhere in the direct vicinity of Loch Ness a well-hidden dragon cult that may have engaged in nothing less than human sacrifice. Cold-blooded murder would be a better description. It would be done with the intention of appeasing those supernatural creatures of the deep. Remarkably, at the end of the twentieth century a very similar story surfaced from England. It suggested the group that Ted Holiday had been pursuing at Loch Ness was actually just a splinter group of a much bigger, possibly even nationwide, organization.

In 2000, Jon Downes and his Center for Fortean Zoology held the first *Weird Weekend* conference in Downes's then home city of Exeter, England. It was a resounding success, to the extent that the annual conference continues to this day. It's very much a family affair where one can hear the latest news, views, and revelations on everything from UFOs to Bigfoot, the Loch Ness Monster to vampires, ghosts to conspiracies. And much more besides. One of those who spoke at the very first weekend was a man named Mike Hallowell, who for some time had been investigating something amazing and controversial in equally mind-bending fashion: the issue of supernatural sacrifice on the east coast of England—and with a sea serpent legend attached to it, no less. Before we get to the heart of the matter, it's worth noting that the waters off the east coast of England are filled with tales of monstrous leviathans. For our purposes, one will suffice.

"It was a most gruesome and thrilling experience"

Filey Brigg is a rocky, impressively sized peninsula that juts out from the coast of the Yorkshire, England, town of Filey. Local folklore suggests that the rocks are actually the remains of the bones of an ancient sea dragon. Unlikely, to say the least. But the story may have at least a basis in reality. In all likelihood, the tale takes its inspiration from centuries-old sightings of giant monsters of the sea that called the crashing waters off Filey Brig their home. One person who was able to attest to this was Wilkinson Herbert, a coastguard, who, in February 1934, had a traumatic, terrifying encounter with just such a sea dragon at Filey Brigg. It was—very appropriately—a dark, cloudy, and windy night when Herbert's life was turned upside down.

The first indication that something foul and supernatural was afoot came when Herbert heard the terrifying growling of what sounded like a dozen or more vicious hounds. The growling, however, was coming from something else entirely. As he looked out at the harsh, cold, waves, Herbert saw—to his terror—a large beast, around thirty feet in length and equipped with a muscular, humped back and four legs that extended into flippers. For a heart-stopping instant, the bright, glowing eyes of the beast locked onto Herbert's eyes. Not surprisingly, he told the *Daily Telegraph* that "it was a most gruesome and thrilling experience. I have seen big animals abroad, but nothing like this."

Further up the same stretch of coastland is the county of Tyne and Wear. And in the vicinity of the county's South Shields is Marsden Bay, an area that is overflowing with rich tales of magic, mystery, witchcraft, and supernatural, ghostly activity. Legend tells of a man named Jack Bates (aka "Jack the Blaster") who, with his wife, Jessie, moved to the area in 1782. Instead of setting up house in the village of Marsden itself, however, the Bates family decided that they would blast a sizable amount of rock out of Marsden Bay and create for themselves a kind of grotto-style home.

It wasn't long before local smugglers saw Jack's cave-like environment as the ideal place to store their goods—something which led Jack to become one of their number. It was a secret working arrangement that existed until the year of Jack the Blaster's death in 1792. The caves were later extended, to the point where they housed, rather astonishingly, a fifteen-room mansion! Today the caves are home to the Marsden Grotto, one of the very few "cave pubs" in Europe. It's very interesting to note that the caves now also harbor portions of the stonework that once comprised Lambton Castle; and that this castle had a monster tradition attached to it, that of the so-called Lambton Worm—which was not at all unlike the famous Linton Worm of Scotland discussed in an earlier chapter. Which brings us now to the heart of the matter: monsters and sacrifice.

Serpents, Sacrifice, and Secrets

With the first *Weird Weekend* of 2000 a resounding success, Jon Downes stayed in touch with Mike Hallowell, who soon revealed something incredible to the monster hunter. Hallowell had been looking into, and had uncovered evidence of, a cult in the area that extended back centuries and which engaged in controversial and dangerous activities. It had all begun with the Viking invasion of the UK in the ninth century and the Norsemen's belief in a violent, marauding sea monster known as the Shoney. Since the Shoney's hunting ground ranged from the coast of England to the waters of Scandinavia and the monster had a reputation for ferociousness, the Vikings did all they could to placate it. That primarily meant providing the beast with certain offerings. We're talking, specifically, about *human* offerings.

The process of deciding who would be the creature's victim was a grim one: the crews of the Viking ships would draw straws and he who drew the shortest straw would be doomed to a terrible fate. He would first be bound by hand and foot. Then, unable to move, he would have his throat violently slashed. After which, the body of the unfortunate soul would be tossed into the churning waters, with the hope that the Shoney would be satisfied and would not attack the Vikings' longships, as they were known. Sometimes the bodies were never seen again. On other occasions they washed up on the shores of Marsden, hideously mutilated and savagely torn to pieces.

Incredibly, however, this was not a practice strictly limited to the long-gone times when the Vikings roamed and pillaged. Mike Hallowell was able to determine that belief in the Shoney never actually died out. As a result, the last such sacrifice was rumored to have occurred in 1928. Hallowell's sources also told him that the grotto caves regularly, and secretly, acted as morgues for the bodies of the dead that the Shoney tossed back onto the beach following each sacrifice.

And now the story becomes even more disturbing: as a dedicated researcher of the unknown, Hallowell began to dig ever deeper into the enigma of Marsden's dragon cult and even contacted local police authorities to try and determine the truth of the matter—and of the murders, too, of course. It was at the height of his research that Hallowell received a number of anonymous phone calls, sternly and darkly warning him to keep away from Marsden and its tale of serpent sacrifice and verbally threatening him as to what might happen if he didn't. To his credit, Hallowell pushed on, undeterred by the Men in Black–like threats. And, although much of the data is circumstantial, Hallowell has made a strong case that such a cult still continues its dark activities—and possibly in other parts of the UK, too.

Finally, it's worth noting that in August 1998 Hallowell, his wife, and his father may have actually seen the Shoney. They were driving along the coast towards Whitburn at the time. In Hallowell's own words, and as they looked towards the sea at Marsden Bay, around ninety feet from the shoreline was "a huge, brown 'thing' breaking the surface of the water. Although only a small 'hump' appeared to be above water level, I could see a much larger area just beneath the surface."

What it was, the three never knew. But the way in which Hallowell found himself personally plunged into the mystery of the Nessie-like Shoney—and at the very same time he was investigating both it and the attendant stories of a dragon cult, to the extent that he even saw the beast—mirrors the situation of Ted Holiday to such a degree that it cannot be coincidence. Rather, it's a case of *when we notice these monstrous things, they notice that we noticed them*, to paraphrase Alan Bates's character, Alexander Leek, in the 2002 movie *The Mothman Prophecies*. They noticed Ted Holiday in 1969—at Loch Ness—and they noticed Mike Hallowell in 1998, at Marsden Bay.

What has largely gone *unnoticed*, however, is the strange wave of encounters with *other* mysterious animals that briefly manifested around Loch Ness in the 2000–2001 period.

27

The *Other* Monsters of Loch Ness

We have previously seen how descriptions of the creatures of Loch Ness vary wildly, from that of a giant frog to a salamander, a gargantuan eel to a plesiosaur, and even a crocodile to a camel-like thing! And let's not forget the tusk-like and turtle-like beasts seen in the loch, too. Clearly, something strange is afoot here, something that may well have a tie-in with the world of shapeshifting—which, as we have also seen, is an integral part of the lore surrounding the kelpie, or water-horse, of the loch. It's a little-known fact, however, that lake monsters are not the only kinds of mysterious creatures seen at Loch Ness.

From 2000 to 2001, the area was hit by a series of sightings of large, unidentified black cats. On May 2, 2000, the *Inverness Courier* newspaper splashed the first such story across its pages. It was a story that provoked a great deal of anxiety and unease amongst the locals, which is not surprising given that the article was titled "Big Cat Sighting Sparks Lambing Time Farm Alert." As the *Courier* noted, it was John Cathcart, a wildlife liaison officer with the Northern Constabulary, who brought the matter to everyone's attention,

prompted by sightings of a puma in the area of Ardersier and of numerous sheep found savagely mutilated and killed.

Two months later, it was Kiltarlity that became the focus for
the savage beast, or of another of its kind. Three sheep were killed
in violent fashion and locals spoke of seeing a huge "panther-like"
animal prowling the landscape by both day and night. One farmer
who was hit hard was Davie MacLean, of Boblainy, who lost two
lambs and a ewe. The heads of the poor animals had been severed from their bodies, their skins lay strewn around the site of
the attack, their ribs were "gnawed bare," and their legs had been
snapped off at the joints. It was a terrifying and traumatic sight for
MacLean.

Then, in September 2001, a similar account reached the staff
of *Nessie's Loch Ness Times*. The witness in this case was one David
Straube, a forestry civil engineering worker who encountered the
creature on the fringes of woods at nearby Huntly. At the time,
Straube was driving his vehicle—and checking the road near
Kinnoir Woods for any defects—when, as he rounded a bend at
approximately 11:30 a.m., he came face to face with a huge black
feline he described as being very much like a puma. It wasted no
time in bounding off into the trees. But not before Straube was
able to take a good look at the animal and fairly conclusively identify it for what it was.

The "Alien Big Cat"/ABC controversy

Sightings of large, unidentified black cats across the British Isles
are not at all uncommon. In fact, quite the opposite: the nation appears to be positively overflowing with such creatures. They have
been reported for decades, and provoke media sensationalism,
public interest and concern, and the occasional dismissive com-

ment from the British Government. They have become known as Alien Big Cats, or ABCs.

Most cryptozoologists suggest that the animals are escapees from private menageries, and the descendants of animals that, back in 1976, were let loose into the wilds of the country after the government changed the laws surrounding the keeping of wild animals. Their names include the Beast of Bodmin, the Surrey Puma, the Chase Panther, the Warrington Lion, and the Beast of Exmoor. Whenever and wherever they are seen, savage mutilations and killings are the norm. Not everyone is quite so sure that the ABCs are what they appear to be, however. Top of the list is Merrily Harpur, the author of *Mystery Big Cats*. She takes the view that the Alien Big Cats may well have supernatural origins, and she just might be right. Encounters with the ABCs very often occur in graveyards, in cemeteries, in the vicinity of stone circles, in ancient burial grounds, and at sites of archaeological and historical significance.

Harpur says that the ABCs are very likely daimons. They are supernatural entities that can be malevolent, helpful, manipulative, trickster-like, and even deadly, depending on their type. Eudemons are generally friendly, while cacodemons should be avoided at all costs lest one wishes to see one's life ruined. As entities that act as intermediaries between the world of man and the domain of the gods, the daimons are shapeshifters that can manifest in multiple forms—such as huge black dogs with blazing red eyes; hideous winged humanoids of a gargoyle-style nature; and … *large black cats*.

Harpur notes, "If ABCs are a variety of native British daimon, they have emerged into a landscape brimful of these intermediate beings: pixies, gnomes, boggarts, Herne the Hunter, elves, lake monsters, 'white ladies,' wyrms, and so on."

That such daimonic entities may have been plaguing the people of Inverness in 2000 and 2001 further bolsters the idea that the monsters of Loch Ness are supernatural in origin. After all, it's not stretching credibility too much to suggest that *one* kind of unknown animal calls the area its home. But *two* kinds? One that lurks in the depths of that legendary loch, and another that slaughters livestock mere miles away? Such an astonishing possibility seems most unlikely in the extreme if we're dealing with regular, flesh-and-blood animals, which does not appear to be the case. And recall that there is the saga of the winged Skree, a hideous monster that manifested right before the Battle of Culloden of 1746, which—geographically-speaking—also has a Loch Ness connection, as we have previously seen.

Wild cats on the shore

It's also notable that the ABCs and lake monsters have turned up at Loch Ness at … *the very same time,* and at *precisely the same locations.* A perfect case in point is an incident that occurred way back in 1658. It's a story that was uncovered by the expert on Scottish lore and legend David Murray Rose, who also penned such titles as *Prince Charlie's Friends* and *Revenue of the Scottish Crown, 1681.* In his letter to the *Scotsman,* Rose commented on the seventeenth-century case of one Sir Ewen Cameron, a resident of Locheil who lived from 1629 to 1719. According to Rose, on one particular day, at the exact time that Cameron was battling with wild cats on a stretch of Loch Ness shoreline, a strange creature was encountered in the Loch: "Old people said it was a 'water-horse' or 'water-kelpie,' because it had a head that looked like a cross between a horse and a camel, but its mouth was in its throat." The story originated with one Patrick Rose of Rosehall, Demerara, who also tackled wild cats at Loch Ness and was given the account of Sir Ewen Cameron by some of the locals.

It should be stressed that Scotland is home to an animal called the Scottish wild cat. Today, sadly, their numbers are few. Fierce and definitely not open to being tamed, they look not unlike regular cats but are slightly bigger. And they won't think twice about severely gashing some inquisitive soul who might get too close.

Perhaps regular wild cats were, indeed, all that Sir Ewen Cameron encountered. On the other hand, the fact that the creatures were seen on the shores of Loch Ness, and that, time-wise, their presence coincided exactly with a sighting of a Nessie, suggests strongly to this author that Cameron may have encountered a band of the far more mysterious, much bigger, and intimidating Alien Big Cats of the daimonic kind.

Moving on from the ABCs, we now turn our attentions to something else; something which demonstrates just how mind-blowingly eerie 2001 was on the Nessie front.

28

Nessie and the White Witch

Two-thousand-and-one was also the year in which one of the strangest, and most surreal of all, supernaturally driven episodes erupted at Loch Ness. Not to mention one of the most entertaining, too. Jan-Ove Sundberg—who, as we saw earlier, claimed an encounter with a landed UFO and its crew at Loch Ness in the summer of 1971—loudly proclaimed that he was going to do something that no one had ever done before: catch a Nessie and present it to the world to see. And it was, hopefully, all going to go down across a specific two-week period in April 2001.

The plan was to try and snare the beast in shallow waters—with a net, no less—and then haul it onto the shore. A most unlikely feat, to say the very least! The British media, always on the lookout for a good new angle on Nessie to talk about, was beyond enthused. They were positively brimming with joy. As a result, it wasn't long before practically the entire nation's newspapers and TV channels were on the story. As was a man named Kevin Carlyon.

A spectral animal from an early era

The "High Priest of British White Witches," Carlyon did not take kindly to the idea of Sundberg snaring a Nessie, and so he decided to do something about it. In April 2001, when Sundberg's monster-grabbing project was planned for, Carlyon did nothing less than come to the rescue of the monsters of Loch Ness. And, as a result, it almost ended in a fistfight between the High Priest himself and Sundberg, and right in the heart of monster-central. Carlyon—a pony-tailed former wrestler—traveled from his home in Hastings, Sussex, England to Scotland. He arrived at Loch Ness dressed in a long, orange-red ceremonial gown and sporting a large five-pointed-star necklace.

With the world of television news filming his every moment, Carlyon, at Temple Pier, began a ritual that was intended to prevent Sundberg from succeeding in his mission to snare a monster. That Carlyon interrupted Sundberg's press conference with the loudly spoken words of "Sundberg be done!" hardly impressed the serpent-seeking Swede. With his anger level growing, Sundberg made loud threats to throw Carlyon into the loch! Carlyon, meanwhile, hit back when Sundberg failed to catch a Nessie by proclaiming that because Sundberg had failed in his goal, his—Carlyon's—magical rite had clearly worked spectacularly well.

A creature-seeker, a magician, and a near-fistfight over a monster: for the media, this was all a dream come true. Indeed, the story even made the BBC news, such was its sheer entertainment value. Independent Television News and Sky News both gave Carlyon substantial coverage, too. Carlyon was not done yet, however. As the day progressed, he took a trip on the loch in *Nessie Hunter*—the boat of a man named George Edwards, a controversy-filled character about whom we will learn a great deal more very soon. Carlyon continued his efforts to protect Nessie from the bad guys (or the bad guy), seeing them come to fruition.

Loch Ness: the site of a magical confrontation in 2001

Carlyon later said that back in 2001, he had an open mind on what the monsters might be. As time progressed, however, and as he spent more and more time at the loch, he came to believe one specific theory: that what lurked in Loch Ness represented something ghostly, a specter from an era long gone. This, you will recall, closely mirrors the conclusions of the U.S. government's remote-viewing team of the 1970s, who speculated that the Loch Ness Monsters possibly represented the spirits of long-dead plesiosaurs. Carlyon added that the beasts appear when "there are certain weather conditions" and "lots of static in the air."

Heading for trouble at the beach

Still in keeping with this curious *Harry Potter*-like state of affairs, there's the matter of Carlyon's connection to another controversial magician, and also in 2001. It's a man whom we have already come to know very well. Kevin Carlyon's hometown in Essex, England, just happens to be *very* close to the town of Hastings—in which Aleister Crowley died on December 1, 1947. Such was the outrage and fear that Crowley provoked, even as late as the 1940s, that the people of Hastings loudly demanded Crowley be buried somewhere else—which he was, in the town of Brighton.

The Crowley-Carlyon link doesn't end there. Just a few miles from Hastings is Beachy Head, a huge cliff face in Eastbourne that has gained notoriety from the large number of suicidal people who, each and every year, throw themselves to their deaths from its 531-feet-above-sea-level height. In 1894, Crowley, a skilled mountaineer, climbed one particularly precarious section of rock-face at Beachy Head. It is known as the Devil's Chimney.

So enamored was he of this deadly but picturesque place, Crowley referred to it as "my grand passion." He added, "The ordinary man looking at a mountain is like an illiterate person confronted with a Greek manuscript. The only chalk in England which is worth reading, so to speak, is that on Beachy Head."

Somewhat embarrassingly, while climbing Old Nick's chimney, Crowley got stuck and incurred the laughter and derision of the locals. Enraged, he cursed them—one and all—stating that when the chimney fell, "all hell, fire and brimstone" would befall the town of Eastbourne. Rather incredibly, it turns out that the Devil's Chimney, a 200-foot-high chalk tower, really *did* collapse—in 2001, the very same year of Kevin Carlyon's ritual at Loch Ness. Thousands of tons of rubble crashed into the rocks below, fortunately injuring or killing no one at all. Who did the fear-filled townsfolk call upon, after the collapse of the chimney, to exorcise the area of any and all Crowley-inspired devilish negativity and to rid them of Crowley's curse? Yes, you've guessed it, Kevin Carlyon, who vowed to perform a "cleansing ceremony" and "dispel any evil."

"The protection will still be there for Nessie"

On June 13, 2003, somewhat amusingly, Carlyon was forced to return to Loch Ness to deal with something unforeseen and amazing. Such was the strong, protective nature of his 2001 spell, it not only prevented Sundberg from catching one of the monsters, but also prevented the Nessies themselves from manifesting! In Carlyon's own words, he had "slightly overdone it," something which allegedly provoked the undeniable drop-off in sightings in the early 2000s. So Carlyon had to, essentially, reduce the power of his spell to ensure that the Nessies could once again travel the deep waters, just as they had for hundreds of years, back to the times when they were known as kelpies and water-horses. With the summer solstice looming large on the horizon, he stood before the loch, specifically a stretch of shore in front of the Clansman Hotel, and cried out loudly, requesting that the loch should once again become the domain of monsters. Carlyon said of his latest actions, "The protection will still be there for Nessie so no one can cause her any harm but she will be able to come back again and thrill the public."

Certainly there is no denying that sightings of the monsters were at an all-time low in the early 2000s—something that made Carlyon's supporters nod knowingly. Yet on one hand, there were three sightings of the Nessies on June 1, which was, of course, twelve days *before* Carlyon reeled in his paranormal power and gave the Nessies their freedom to roam again. Even so, there was talk of the possibility that since Carlyon's plans to return to the loch actually predated June 1, his supernatural skills were already having a positive effect on the Nessie presence, in ripple-effect-style, before he actually arrived there.

The witch returns—again

Carlyon is clearly someone who enjoys, and basks in, the limelight aspect of the Nessie controversy, as much as he does in the mystery itself. And there's nothing wrong with that. As evidence of this, in 2006 Carlyon was yet again back at Loch Ness, and again whipping up controversy and keeping the media more than happy in the process. It was the morning of Sunday, January 15, and Carlyon was on the shore of the loch with "many of my Scottish witches," where he accepted the "gracious title" of "The Official Protector and High Priest of Loch Ness." One day later, Britain's Channel 4 interviewed him for their *Morning Glory* show. It was an interview that was beset by endless problems with the crew's electrical equipment. As we know, such problems very often surface in the vicinity of paranormal monsters, whether Nessie, Bigfoot, or Mothman. It was, said Carlyon, as if the equipment had been "drained of energy." Maybe he was right on target.

Adding to the publicity factor of the affair, Carlyon said that he intended to write to the British Prime Minister at the time, Tony Blair, and have him officially change the name of the Loch Ness Monster to that of the far less atmospheric Loch Ness Creature. And if he failed to receive a reply from Blair, Carlyon continued, "he will only remain Prime Minister for a short 'spell.'" Carlyon didn't receive a reply, and Blair was voted out of office in 2007. Coincidence, or the magic might of Carlyon? As long as the newspapers were around to comment on the affair, and comment at length, it scarcely mattered. Except to the Nessies, perhaps.

One suspects we have not heard the last of Kevin Carlyon and his Loch Ness escapades. No doubt the BBC is waiting with eager, bated breath. Maybe the monsters of the loch are, too.

As strange as the Carlyon-Sundberg situation was, it couldn't hold a candle to what happened in 2007.

29

A Controversy Caught on Camera

In 2007, one of the most amazing and significant encounters in a very long time occurred at Loch Ness. It was an encounter that had both the Nessie-based research community and monster hunters everywhere practically foaming at the mouth with excitement. This was hardly surprising, since the witness in question, a lab technician named Gordon Holmes, succeeded in filming one of the world-famous legendary beasts. And this was not a piece of vague or blurry footage of a questionable nature; it was there, clear enough for anyone and everyone to see. Cryptozoologists quickly and loudly championed the film, confident that this was just the latest in a long line of evidence demonstrating that monsters of a flesh-and-blood and unidentified nature dwelled deep in Loch Ness's waters.

As the media and the creature-seeking crowd began to dig further, however, something both remarkable and controversial surfaced. Namely, evidence that Gordon Holmes, of Shipley, Yorkshire, England, had a lifetime of supernatural and paranormal activity and encounters. In other words, for Holmes, the Nessie encounter was just the latest in a series of extensive unexplainable incidents. It wasn't long at all before the flesh-and-blood brigade were at major loggerheads with the paranormally inclined. With that said, let's take a look at the strange saga of Gordon Holmes, and how and why his encounter with a Loch Ness Monster only serves to increase the suspicions that the animals are supernatural in nature.

Filming a monster

Around 10:00 p.m. on May 26, 2007, Holmes filmed, well, *something* in Loch Ness. It was something that turned him into an overnight media sensation—albeit a brief one. The day in question was dominated by heavy rain, but which cleared as the evening arrived, allowing Holmes to get clear footage of what looked like some kind of animal moving at significant knots in the waters of Loch Ness. The specific location from where all the action was captured was a parking area on the A82 road, just a couple of miles from Drumnadrochit. Not only that, but Holmes estimated, as he excitedly watched and filmed, that the creature was around fourteen meters in length—which, if true, effectively ruled out *everything* known to live in the inland waters of the British Isles.

Holmes and his near-priceless film were quickly big news, catching the attention of not just the British media, but also the likes of NBC News and CNN. When the media descended upon him in absolute droves, Holmes said that he had scarcely believed what he was seeing. It was a large, black-colored animal that had a length of around forty-five feet. His first thought was of a giant eel. Holmes told NBC News of the eel theory: "They have serpent-like features and they may explain all the sightings in Loch Ness over the years."

Long-time Nessie seeker Adrian Shine was moved to comment in a fairly positive fashion. Although describing himself as a skeptic on matters concerning the monsters, Shine was certainly no debunker of this latest case. Indeed, when interviewed by NBC, he said of Gordon Holmes's film that it was "some of the best footage I have seen." Shine was careful to add that while Holmes might have filmed a living beast, there was always a possibility that the whole thing could be explained away by waves, or that it might well have been a case of seeing something we wanted to see and then interpreted it as a monster—whatever "it" really was.

It wasn't long before monster hunters turned their attentions away from the Loch Ness Monster and in the direction of Holmes himself, something which provoked huge controversies when certain eye-opening and eyebrows-raising issues came to light.

From Merlin's meteorite
to a Neolithic solstice

Cryptozoologist Loren Coleman discovered that Holmes had a biographical page at the Department of Archaeological Sciences at Bradford University, on which he was described as holding the position of Media and IT Technician. Nothing wrong with that, of course. But there was more to come. In addition, Coleman demonstrated that Holmes had written a number of books, including *The Complex Creation of All Universes*; *2000 BC: A Neolithic Solstice Odyssey*; and *Merlin's Meteorite*. Rather intriguingly, Holmes himself said that his then most recent book, *Trice Visualisation*, "describes a sort of medical condition I have for visualizing a sort of frame from a dream whilst being conscious." The images he saw typically lasted for under a minute, and occurred every two or three months.

Did Holmes's seemingly psychic skills give him the ability to see, and even film, one of the supernatural Nessies on that fateful night in May 2007? It's a controversial theory we should not rule out. And the controversy didn't end there. It had scarcely gotten started.

Fairies and a stone circle

In 2001, much of the UK's cattle herd was decimated by a devastating outbreak of foot and mouth disease. More than ten million sheep and cattle were put to death. It was around the time when the crisis came to an end—in September 2001—that Holmes had an encounter with *another* unknown animal that has been seen at Loch Ness. It was one of the mysterious Alien Big Cats, or ABCs, that Merrily Harpur believes to be body-morphing daimons. The location of Holmes's encounter was the little hamlet of Newby Cote, near Clapham, Yorkshire Dales—where the ABC was stalking a group of frightened sheep. Holmes also claimed to have photographed fairies, at a place called Load Saddle Well on the wilds of Ilkley Moor, England—an area renowned for its many and varied encounters of the UFO kind, and near to what is called the Twelve Apostles. An ancient circle of standing stones, the Twelve Apostles was constructed during the Bronze Age. It was things like this that led Loren Coleman to say, "Realistically, we must now admit, at the very least, Gordon T. Holmes is a bit eccentric." Or maybe he wasn't.

Having an effect on reality

Many within the monster-hunter community felt that Holmes's claims to have seen both fairies and an alien big cat impacted deeply and negatively on his film footage of an alleged Loch Ness Monster. Of course, it only impacts negatively if one rigidly holds to the theory that the Nessies are biological, flesh-and-blood animals. If, as this book suggests time and again, the creatures are not what they appear to be, then Holmes's claims may not be so outlandish after all. They just might be right on the money.

Let's look at the facts: Holmes undeniably filmed something of paramount importance, something which caught the attention of the world's mainstream media. Even Adrian Shine was not unimpressed by it. In that sense, the film has fairly significant credentials. Let's not forget, too, that Holmes claimed the psychic ability to visualize "a sort of frame" from a dream "whilst being conscious." In other words, Holmes may have been able to have an impact on, even affect, what we term reality.

The nature of reality, remember, was something that Tim Dinsdale and Ted Holiday pondered extensively in the 1970s when confronted by the undeniably stranger aspects of the Nessie affair. And if Holmes's abilities allowed him to see one supernatural monster, perhaps that is why he was also able to catch sight of yet another monster: a daimonic alien big cat. Plus, Holmes's alleged encounter with fairies occurred at the site of an English stone circle. As we have seen, Loch Ness has its very own stone circle controversy, concerning those formations discovered in 1976 and dubbed the Kleinhenges.

So, what we have with Gordon Holmes is a man who filmed a Loch Ness Monster, who possessed unusual psychic abilities, and who—probably as a result of those same abilities—was able to tap into a strange, ethereal, and usually unseen realm dominated by *other* monsters and fabulous magical creatures, too.

Gordon Holmes's film, in relation to the Loch Ness Monster, was the undeniable highlight of the first decade of the twenty-first century. That the footage, the man who shot the film, and just about every attendant aspect of the story was steeped in matters of a supernatural nature demonstrates something notable: that very little had changed since the turbulent and terror-filled days of the early-to-mid 1970s, when Ted Holiday was plunged into equally weird situations of the supernatural kind.

Another thing that hadn't changed was Doc Shiels's connection to the world of lake monsters. A certain series of events that occurred in 2009 makes that very obvious.

Doc Shiels and even more lake monsters

In the summer of 1994, Jonathan Downes, of the Center for Fortean Zoology, traveled to London to attend the first conference organized by the staff of the British newsstand magazine *Fortean Times*—a glossy monthly journal dedicated to just about anything and everything of a paranormal nature. The Unconvention, as it is known, was a resounding success and attracted an impressively sized audience. It's an event that is still held to this very day. For Downes the event was particularly notable, since he met, for the first time, the almost legendary Tony "Doc" Shiels. By Downes's own admission, a great deal of Guinness and whisky was drunk at the conference, at the end of which Downes and Shiels were firm friends, if slightly pickled ones. That friendship continues today, despite a few rocky moments over the years.

On a particular September day, fifteen years after that very first meeting, Downes, his wife, Corinna, and CFZ colleague Max Blake found themselves on the shore of Ireland's Lough Leane. This was, recall, the site of Doc Shiels's monster-raising activity in 1981, and where the mysterious Patrick Kelly claimed to have seen and photographed a serpentine lake-beastie. It was late afternoon on September 17, and Doc had invited the trio to spend some time with him. Notably, Shiels said that the trio of creature-seekers should keep their eyes focused on one particular stretch of water. As Corinna notes, something very strange appeared before them: "I saw a trail left by something as it made its way from the island to the shore to the east of it ... I was to be pressed for an answer I would probably suggest a large eel." Max Blake recorded his thoughts on the encounter, too: "If I had to make a guess, I would say that it was most likely to have been a giant eel."

Corinna Downes and Max Blake may indeed be correct in their shared theory that the creature which all four saw was an eel of immense proportions. It is, however, notable that Shiels specifically directed the three creature-seekers to keep their eyes on one specific portion of Lough Leane, and specifically *before* anything unusual occurred. And sure enough, lo and behold, and within mere minutes, something unusual duly manifested for one and all. It was fortuitous, indeed, that Downes had accepted Shiels's invite.

Those of a skeptical mindset may say that this was all the result of a coincidence. Or that a giant eel, of previously unheard-of proportions, just happened to appear at the very same time that the Center for Fortean Zoology was on-site to encounter it. A far more plausible theory, however, is that this was yet another example of Doc Shiels invoking a supernatural lake monster and the creature duly appearing—this time for Shiels's three visiting friends from England. Exactly as Shiels had done at Loch Ness back in 1977.

30

The Loch Ness Aliens
—and a Hoax

More Loch Ness weirdness hit the news in 2011, specifically in August of that year. The UK's *Daily Express* newspaper splashed a headline across its pages that read, "Alert as UFO is sighted over Loch Ness." The story was, undoubtedly, an odd one. That something actually occurred does not appear to be in doubt; the nature of the "something" is what remains open to debate. It was on the night of August 20, 2011, that a number of people—many being completely independent of each other—encountered an unusual object in the skies over Loch Ness. Witness descriptions of the object's movements fell into two camps: those who said they saw it descending into the loch, and those who maintained it was hovering above the expansive waters. As for a description of the UFO, it very much depended on whom one asked. Yet whatever it was, it quickly caught the attention of the emergency services, who were contacted by worried locals.

Martin Douglas, of the Loch Ness Life Boat crew, told the *Daily Mail* that someone in the area had seen what, superficially at least, resembled a microlight or a hang glider, which actually seemed to enter the loch in a controlled flight. Oddly, however, others who saw the unknown craft described it as being somewhat balloon-shaped. Then there were those who opined it looked eerily like a fully-open parachute. There was, then, no solid consensus on what was seen—or on what wasn't seen. Crew member Vivian Bailey added that although the mystery was not resolved, the emergency services were pleased that concerned people had quickly contacted them.

There is, however, a very odd afterword to all this.

Exactly one month previously, on July 21, law enforcement offices in North America, in the vicinity of 125-mile-long Lake Champlain—which covers parts of New York and Vermont, as well as portions of Quebec, Canada—were inundated with calls from worried locals, all of whom had seen a balloon-like object fall into the huge lake near Rouses Point, New York. Police and Border Patrol personnel were quickly dispatched to scour the area, but with no luck. After around four hours, the search was called off. It remained a mystery. It should be noted, however, that just like Loch Ness, Lake Champlain has its own resident monster. Champ, as the creature is famously known, is, like Nessie, a large, long-necked leviathan that has taken on near-legendary proportions.

Is it only coincidence that two lakes on opposite sides of the world—both with resident monsters—should have been the sites of unusual, and very similar, UFO-like activity within a month of each other? Or is this yet further evidence of profound paranormal weirdness wherever lake monsters lurk?

"The best photograph I think I have ever seen"

If for nothing else when it comes to Nessie, 2012 will be remembered as the year of an audacious and embarrassing hoax. It was a hoax which led one of the leading figures in Nessie research to make a rash statement of support that came back to haunt him. The person behind the ruse—or, more to the point, the "faker" and "liar," as he was soon termed—was a man named George Edwards. He operates a cruise service to people traveling the loch, whether for business or pleasure or to search for the monsters. Edwards briefly became the subject of near-worldwide news in 2012 when he released a photograph that appeared to show the large hump of an unknown animal protruding prominently out of the waters of Loch Ness. In days—maybe hours—the photo was splashed just about everywhere. This was finally it; the proof monster-hunters everywhere had been waiting for.

As recounted the following year in the *Telegraph*, Steve Feltham, one of the Nessie seekers most committed to finding the truth, had stated that Edwards's picture was "the best photograph I think I have ever seen . . . I think the images are fantastic—that's the animal I have been looking for all this time." Feltham had had even more to say on the matter of the picture. While he admitted that it didn't offer any meaningful, concrete data on what the Nessies are, he did state that the photo made it abundantly clear that they were not large fish, such as sturgeon. Those were pretty eye-opening statements, ones that a lot of creature seekers sat up and took notice of. It was, however, all just too good to be true.

"Why should I feel guilty for having a bit of fun?"

In August 2012, when Edwards revealed his photograph for one and all to see, he said that he'd held back on revealing it for a while, chiefly because he wanted to make certain he had captured something genuinely anomalous—and not something down to earth, such as a large rotting log. Edwards even claimed that the photo had been studied by certain elements of the U.S. military. He added, "I was really excited as I am sure that some strange creatures are lurking in the depths of Loch Ness."

The Nessie-hunting community was intrigued and enthusiastic and began to dig further into Edwards's claims and photo. That's when alarm bells began to ring. They were soon ringing at ear-splitting levels. It wasn't long before the community was able to demonstrate that the large, rounded back in Edwards's photo closely—as in near-identically—resembled a carbon-fiber hump that had been used in a 2011 National Geographic Channel show titled *The Truth Behind the Loch Ness Monster*. There was a good reason for the resemblance: they were one and the same! Edwards had been in the show and had access to the model. He finally confessed in 2013, telling the *Telegraph*:

"Why should I feel guilty for having a bit of fun? These so-called experts come along with their theories about big waves and big fish, and their visitor centre, but I'm sick to death of them."

Steve Feltham hit back at Edwards, noting—correctly—that orchestrated hoaxes achieve nothing positive, have a negative effect on the search for the Nessies, and destroy reputations. Bristling with anger, Feltham was quoted as calling Edwards "nothing more than a faker and a liar."

Feltham's words got a great deal of coverage. The damage, however, was already done, and, in the eyes of many, Nessie had suffered a severe blow to its credibility. This didn't keep the UFOs away, however. In 2015—according to some, at least—they were back.

UFOs caught on film?

In the summer of 2015, the controversy of the Loch Ness Monster was taken to a new height—as in literally. That was when the mystery was yet again linked to the matter of high-flying UFOs. As we have already seen, there is nothing new about a Nessie-UFO link:

Jan-Ove Sundberg claimed an encounter with a landed unidentified flying object at Loch Ness in 1971; Ted Holiday had a sighting of a menacing Man in Black at the loch three years later; and in August 2011, numerous people caught sight of an unidentified flying object over the waters of Loch Ness. The 2015 affair was but yet another weird addition to the Nessie mystery.

The three key players in the story, according to the *Mirror*, were Alan Betts and his wife, Anna, and Anna's mother, Tatiana. The family, from the English city of York, were holidaying in Scotland. It was April 2015, and the three were staying at a cottage near Urquhart Castle—which, as has been demonstrated in these pages, is an undeniable hot spot for Nessie encounters. While at the loch, as is the case for practically everyone who visits, they took a good number of photos. It wasn't until the Betts returned home, however, that they realized just how weird one of their vacation pictures was. Taken by Tatiana, it appeared to show a pair of anomalous objects in the sky right over Loch Ness. As if Nessie wasn't enough of a mystery on its own!

"Our Akita dog, Yuka, was strangely unsettled that night"

Alan—the director of a refrigerating company—said when the story hit the headlines two months later that the timing of their vacation had been fortuitous. The weather was pretty much perfect: that is to say, it was bright and sunny for almost their entire visit. However, on one particular day, after the Betts spent hours checking out the area, things changed. The sunny weather was suddenly gone and everything quickly became dark and gloomy, the rain pouring down in definitive deluge style. Tatiana decided to take a photo of the moody skies—something which proved to be crucial to the story. It was when they downloaded their holiday pictures onto their PC that they noticed something odd in that particular photo. It was a pair of brightly lit objects that appeared to be flying over Loch Ness, but which nobody saw at the time Tatiana took the picture. Alan, despite being a self-confessed skeptic, admitted that he was at a loss to explain what the camera had captured. Interestingly, he added, "Our Akita dog, Yuka, was strangely unsettled that night."

Anna, when approached by the *Huffington Post* for comment on the growing controversy surrounding the photo, said, "We can say 100 percent that the camera was perfectly fine. It was raining very heavily, there were no lights in the house to resemble the objects in any shape or form."

While no one suggested that the Betts had deliberately faked the photo—not even the skeptics believed that—some commentators suspected that the entire matter could be explained away via light reflection. Both Anna and Alan felt that such an explanation was unlikely, noting that no lights were on when the picture was taken.

And, at the time of this writing, that's pretty much where things still stand. The Betts are sure they photographed something unusual, while the skeptics are positive the case can be explained in wholly rational terms.

31

A Change of Mind and Monster-Fish

Shock waves reverberated throughout the Loch Ness Monster-seeking community in July 2015, when the UK media reported on something sensational. Steve Feltham announced that close to a quarter of a century after moving to Loch Ness, he had come to the conclusion that there were no Loch Ness Monsters at all. Instead, there were catfish. Or even, perhaps, just *one* Loch Ness catfish; a very large and extremely old one. Given that Feltham had championed the monster for years, this was not good news for those who flew the flag of Nessie. Before we get to the heart of the story, though, let's head back a couple of decades, to the time when Feltham decided to leave the world of nine to five and devote himself to the study of the world's most famous lake monster of all.

Until 1991, Steve Feltham lived a relatively normal life. He had a home, a girlfriend, and a job as an installer of security systems. Then everything changed. Having been fascinated by the saga of Nessie since he was a child, Feltham left his girlfriend and his home, quit his job, and moved to live in a trailer—actually, a converted mobile library—on the shores of Loch Ness. Today, the trailer stands on the car park of a nearby pub. As for Feltham's one and only source of income? It's the models he makes of Nessie, which pay the bills and put food on the table. Such is the extensive period of time Feltham has been in residence at Loch Ness—twenty-four years, at the time of this writing—that he even has his very own place in the Guinness Book of Records for "the longest monster hunting vigil of the Loch."

Feltham dedicated his days, nights, weeks, months, years, and, finally, decades to seeking out the truth of the Nessies. And while his quest continues, it was in the summer of 2015 that his views on Nessie changed. And changed radically, given that what for Feltham was once something fantastic and monstrous is now nothing stranger than an oversized catfish. The media had a field day with this, while Nessie fans shook their heads in disbelief and fellow creature-seekers worried that the Nessie mystery was about to come crashing down around them.

The idea that the Loch Ness Monsters might be catfish is not a new one. To a degree, the theory isn't out of the question for at least *some* reports. The specific kind of catfish that Feltham had in mind was the Wels catfish, which is native to much of Europe as well as to the Caspian, Baltic, and Black Seas. While most Wels catfish grow to lengths of around five feet, there are reports of them extending to around ten feet in length, and very occasionally even longer, possibly to roughly thirteen feet in some cases. Claims of sixteen-foot-long catfish have been made, although they are, admittedly, unverified. Nevertheless, there's little doubt that the UK *is* home to large catfish.

Chasing a monster-fish

In 2002, Jon Downes wrote a book titled *Monster of the Mere*. It was a study of the Center for Fortean Zoology's investigation, in that year, of a large catfish that lurked in Martin Mere, in the county of Lancashire, England. The investigation was one that caught the attention of the nation's media, which followed the CFZ on just about each and every aspect of the expedition. After spending extensive time at the mere, team member Richard Freeman saw the beast up close and personal. In his book, Downes recounts the July 26, 2002, words of Freeman:

"At around nine in the evening on the first night … I saw a portion of the back of a large fish that appeared to be basking in the shallows. It was oily black in color and bore a dorsal crest … Gauging the size of the animal was hard as only a small area of its back was visible, but judging by the disturbance it caused it must have been substantial."

Freeman had one more brief encounter with the creature, which left him in no doubt that something of a notable size was swimming within Martin Mere.

"I was really shaken up by it"

In June 2015, a huge fish was spotted by two astonished and terrified anglers on the River Nene, in the Fens, Cambridgeshire, England. One of the fishermen told BBC Radio Cambridgeshire that on the day when all hell broke loose, the two friends were boating in the direction of Whittlesey when their boat juddered—suggesting they had collided with something. But with what? They peered over the side of the boat and encountered something extraordinary: a huge fish, easily six feet in length and possibly even slightly bigger, swimming by. While they weren't sure of the specific type of fish, there is no denying it was a definitive monster, and hardly the kind of thing one would normally expect to see in the River Nene—or in any other stretch of English water.

The two men speculated that what they had seen was a sturgeon. Not an impossibility, since sturgeon can grow to impressive sizes. But the catfish was also offered as a potential candidate—echoing both the Center for Fortean Zoology's experiences at Martin Mere in 2002 and the 2015 theories of Steve Feltham regarding the Loch Ness Monsters.

Then there was the theory of another witness—namely that the creature was not a catfish but a giant eel, a creature that, as demonstrated in the pages of this book, has often been suggested for the Loch Ness Monsters. That witness was forty-one-year-old Michelle Cooper, who was prompted to come forward by the media publicity given to the fishermen's encounter. Her sighting in the River Nene, however, had occurred approximately one year earlier. She told the *Cambridge News* that some of her friends poked fun at her when she told them of her encounter with the mysterious leviathan. But Cooper was sure that what she saw was something huge and daunting. She was terrified by it, too. Notably, while speaking with the media, she noted that "when I researched what it could [be] I found it looked exactly like the giant eels you get in America. I was really shaken up by it."

Although Michelle Cooper was sure that what she had seen was not a catfish but an eel of a gargantuan size, it was specifically this report—along with that of the anglers—that reignited the catfish debate concerning the Loch Ness Monster. It's not entirely improbable, therefore, that this debate may have stirred Steve Feltham to reconsider his stance on the nature of the Nessies. Even if this was not the case, the timing is curious, since it was merely weeks later that Feltham went public and blew the long-held exotic theories right out of the water.

Analyzing the catfish

While Feltham's statement concerning what we might call the "Loch Ness Catfish" certainly made massive waves—no pun intended—there are certain issues that need to be addressed. Yes, the back of a significantly sized catfish might very well be mistaken for a genuinely unknown creature in Loch Ness. A catfish, however, offers no explanation for the famous long neck of Nessie. Nor can it explain the front and back flippers. On the matter of the monsters of Loch Ness being seen on land, things are admittedly a bit more problematic. As incredible as it might sound, there actually is one type of catfish that can exit the water and walk on land, in wiggly, snake-like movements. Its name is *Clarias batrachus*, or "the walking catfish." It uses its pectoral fins—located on both sides of its body—to force itself along, for up to no less than several hours out of the water.

However, what is problematic is the fact that *Clarias Batrachus* is native to Southeast Asia, and *only* to Southeast Asia. Plus it rarely grows beyond one and a half feet in length and typically weighs a mere two and a half pounds when fully grown. Thus if the Nessies are giant catfish, and the land-based encounters are valid, then we must be dealing with catfish of a completely unknown variety, which, for some unfathomable reason, grew to massive lengths in Loch Ness and—a few more Scottish lochs aside, such as Loch Morar—nowhere else on the planet.

There is also the matter of a statement from Feltham to the *Daily Mail* that "it is known they [catfish] were introduced into English lakes by the Victorians for sport." That's true. One glaring problem with these words, however, is that, as we saw in the opening pages of this book, sightings of the Nessies date back to the sixth century. The catfish theory, therefore, leaves much to be desired when it comes to all the pre-nineteenth-century, pre-Victorian-era reports.

While the media lapped up Feltham's words in eager fashion, as well as the possibility that a catfish or several may have been responsible for some Nessie encounters, overall the theory fails as a result of its undeniable inability to explain the many facets of Nessie—and, most obviously, the long necks of the creatures. Something the media oddly avoided commenting on.

Having now analyzed myriad inexplicable encounters with this creature, from the sixth century to the present day, it is time to form some conclusions on the strange matter of the world's most supernatural monster.

Conclusions

Our strange and at times turbulent story is finally at its end. As we have seen, time and again, the *real* story of the Loch Ness Monster is very different from the one that has been presented by countless cryptozoologists and monster hunters over the years and decades. It's also a story that many of those same cryptozoologists and monster hunters have clearly ignored. Or perhaps even deliberately suppressed. This is evidenced by the fact that the supernatural data is out there, to be seen by one and all, yet it has barely been touched upon at length or discussed in the vast majority of Nessie-themed books.

The reason why it has been ignored is abundantly obvious: mainstream cryptozoology does not wish to see the down-to-earth theories challenged by the world of the paranormal. I understand that cherished beliefs which suggest the Nessies are plesiosaurs are important to many. However, ignoring key data will not help solve the mystery. In reality, such an approach will have the polar opposite effect: it will stifle research and push it down the wrong road.

Time and again, we have seen the monsters of Loch Ness tied to the domain of the supernatural. No less than the very first recorded sighting—the sixth-century affair of St. Columba—was steeped in strange phenomena. The monster's deadly games were reeled in by the saint, who called upon the power of the Christian god to try and rein in the creature.

More than a thousand years later, the monster was still plaguing the people of Loch Ness. That much is made clear by the tales of the kelpies of the loch. It's important to note that not one solitary soul believed them to be regular, albeit unknown, animals. Indeed, the unanimous conclusion was that the kelpies were deadly, paranormal monsters that had the ability to alter their physical appearances. Such theories, and fears, extended right up until the final years of the nineteenth century—and made a resurgence years later, largely thanks to the work of Ted Holiday. And also regarding the final years of the 1800s, there is the not-insignificant fact that none other than the "Great Beast," Aleister Crowley, lived at Loch Ness's Boleskine House. That Crowley—deliberately, inadvertently, or a bit of both—conjured up infernal, supernatural entities and helped create an air of malignant menace at the loch cannot be denied, and cannot be without relevance.

Something else which cannot be denied is the fact that when the term "Loch Ness Monster" was created in the 1930s, it prompted a multitude of reports that described the Nessies in wildly varying ways. Arthur Grant encountered a monster with distinct flippers and a long neck. Hugh Gray's famous photo shows a creature that pretty much lacks *any* kind of neck; as for its head, it is beak-like. Lieutenant McP Fordyce's monster had long legs (rather than flippers), walked on the land, and was somewhat hairy, rather than dark and serpent-like. Add to that the tusked and frog-like Nessies of earlier years and what we have is a modern incarnation of the old kelpie—a creature that could morph into multiple forms. The implication is obvious: the kelpies of old never really went away. They were merely upgraded for new generations and given a new name: Nessie.

The highly bizarre, and downright sinister, situations into which the ill-fated Ted Holiday found himself plunged are further evidence of the supernatural forces that lurk and manipulate at Loch Ness. Men in Black, strange synchronicities, the mysterious and deadly dragon cult, the Reverend Donald Omand's exorcism, repeated encounters near creepy old Urquhart Castle, and Holiday's very own unrelenting descent into a word filled with magic, mysticism, and the occult all make that clear. Even Tim Dinsdale—hardly publicly known for believing in the supernatural nature of the monsters—admitted to having crossed paths with certain paranormal aspects of the Nessie mystery. Let's not forget, too, that when all manner of high-strangeness and "dragon-raising" were afoot at Loch Ness in 1968 and 1969, there was also a sudden resurgence of sightings of Morag, the beast of Loch Morar.

The undeniable UFO-themed aspects of the Loch Ness Monster controversy are clear to see, too. As are the varied encounters of the ghostly variety at the loch, such as the one involving St. Columba's boat and the Second World War–era crash of a Wellington bomber aircraft. Add to that the odd story of the Kleinhenges; the U.S. government's remote viewers and their "Nessie is a ghost" theory; those mysterious, large, daimonic black cats seen at Loch Ness; the intriguing film footage taken in 2007 by Gordon Holmes, a man deeply linked to psychic forces; and the actions of the "High Priest of British White Witches," Kevin Carlyon. What we have, combined, is a perspective on Loch Ness, and its resident monsters, that takes us just about as far away as possible from the world of zoology—known or unknown.

Make no mistake, the Loch Ness Monsters are real. They exist. It is the nature of that reality, and the nature of that existence, that so many need to come to grips with and learn to accept. Yes, we really *are* dealing with monsters in those dark depths. That much must, by now, be obvious to all but the most feebleminded. And as just about every aspect of this book has demonstrated, monsters are not merely what they appear to be. They are, in fact, far worse and much stranger ...

Bibliography

Adomnán of Iona. *Life of St. Columba.* London: Penguin Classics, 1995.

Ailes, Emma. "Loch Ness Monster: Is Nessie Just a Tourist Conspiracy?" BBC News, April 14, 2013. http://www.bbc.com /news/uk-scotland-22125981.

"Aleister Crowley." Thelemapedia, April 2, 2011. http://www .thelemapedia.org/index.php/Aleister_Crowley.

"Analysis of the Tim Dinsdale Film." Legend of Nessie, 2009. http://www.nessie.co.uk/htm/the_evidence/analysis.html.

Apiryon, T. "Sir Edward Kelly," Ordo Templi Orientis, 1995. The Hermetic Library. http://hermetic.com/sabazius/kelly.htm.

Arnold, Neil. "Stig of the Dump and Its Crypto-Connections." Still On the Track: The Voice of the International Zoological Community, December 21, 2010. http://forteanzoology .blogspot.com/2010/12/neil-arnold-stig-of-dump-and-its -crypto.html.

Ascher-Walsh, Rebecca. "George Sanders' Suicide." Entertainment, May 8, 1992. http://www.ew.com/article/1992/05/08 /george-sanders-suicide.

Baker, Keiligh. "Is This the Loch Ness ALIEN? Holidaymaker Captures Extraordinary Photo of Strange Disc-shaped UFO in the Highlands." *Daily Mail*, June 10, 2015. http://www .dailymail.co.uk/news/article-3118300/Holidaymaker -captures-photo-disc-shaped-UFO-Loch-Ness.html.

Baker, Keiligh, and James Dunn. "Loch Ness Expert Who Has Spent 24 Years Watching for Nessie and Even Lost His Girl-friend and Home Says He Now Believes It Is Nothing But a CATFISH." *Daily Mail*, July 15, 2015. http://www.dailymail .co.uk/news/article-3162580/Loch-Ness-expert-believes -CATFISH.html.

Baumann, Elwood D. *The Loch Ness Monster*. New York, NY: Franklin Watts, Inc., 1972.

Beach Combing. "Did You Hear the One About Nessie, the Sceptic and the Water Horse?" Beachcombing's Bizarre History Blog, February 2, 2014. http://www.strangehistory.net /2014/02/02/15035.

Belekurov, Shaun. "Is the Loch Ness Monster a Shapeshifter?" *Paranormal Underground*, Vol. 3, Issue 7, July 2010.

Bender, Albert. *Flying Saucers and the Three Men*. New York: Paperback Library, Inc., 1968.

"Big Foot." Legendary Dartmoor. March 25, 2016. http://www .legendarydartmoor.co.uk/big_foot.htm.

"Boblainy Beast Strikes." *Kiltarlity News*, Issue 11, July 2000.

Boese, Alex. "The Surgeon's Photo." The Museum of Hoaxes, 2015. http://hoaxes.org/photo_database/image/the_surgeons_photo.

Bord, Janet, and Colin Bord. *Alien Animals*. Harrisburg, PA: Stackpole Books, 1981.

Brown, Raymond. "'Terrifying' Mystery Monster Lurking in Cambridgeshire River Now Sighted Twice Could Be Giant Eel."

Cambridge News, June 25, 2015. http://www.cambridge-news
.co.uk/mystery-monster-lurking-cambridgeshire-river
/story-26766152-detail/story.html.

Burns, Robert. "Address to the Devil." 1786. Poetry Foundation,
2015. http://www.poetryfoundation.org/poem/173053.

Cady, Brian. "The Private Life of Sherlock Holmes." TCM.com,
2016. http://www.tcm.com/this-month/article/33762|0/The
-Private-Life-of-Sherlock-Holmes.html.

Campell, Alex. "Strange Spectacle on Loch Ness—What Was It?"
Inverness Courier, May 2, 1933.

Campbell, Elizabeth Montgomery, and David Solomon. *The Search
for Morag*. London: Tom Stacey, 1972.

Campbell, J. F. *Popular Tales of the West Highlands*. 4 vol. Edinburgh:
Edmonston & Douglas, 1860–1862.

Carlyon, Kevin. "The Loch Ness Creature 2006." http://www
.kevincarlyon.co.uk/channel4lochness.html. Accessed 2015.

Carmichael, Alexander. *Carmina Gadelica: Hymns and Incantations,
Vol. II*. Edinburgh, Scotland: T. & A. Constable, 1900.

Caro, G.B. "Boleskine House, The Home of the Wickedest Man
in the World." Murder is Everywhere, July 19, 2013. http://
murderiseverywhere.blogspot.com/2013/07/boleskin-house
-home-of-wickedest-man-in.html.

"Catfish Families & Groups." All Catfish Species Inventory. http://
silurus.acnatsci.org/ACSI/taxa/Families.html. Accessed 2015.

Churton, Tobias. *Aleister Crowley, the Beast in Berlin*. Rochester, VT:
Inner Traditions, 2014.

"Clava Cairns." Historic Environment Scotland. http://www
.historic-scotland.gov.uk/propertyresults/propertydetail.htm
?PropID=PL_067. Accessed 2015.

Coleman, Loren. "Nessie Footage Questions Focus On Film-maker." Cryptomundo, June 4, 2007. http://cryptomundo.com /cryptozoo-news/holmes-concern.

———. "Strange Objects Over Lake Champlain and Loch Ness." Cryptomundo, August 22, 2007. http://cryptomundo.com /cryptozoo-news/ufos-lochlake.

———. "Was Arthur Grant's Nessie Encounter Fact or Fiction?" Cryptomundo, November 19, 2011. http://cryptomundo.com /cryptozoo-news/grant-ln.

———. "The Water Horse Land Sightings at Loch Ness." Crypto-zoonews, December 22, 2007. http://www.cryptozoonews .com/ness-land.

Coleman, Loren, and Patrick Huyghe. *The Field Guide to Lake Monsters, Sea Serpents, and Other Mysterious Denizens of the Deep*. San Antonio, TX: Anomalist Books, 2003.

Collins, Andrew. *The New Circlemakers: Insights Into the Crop Circle Mystery*. Virginia Beach, VA: A.R.E. Press, 2009.

"The Confessions of Aleister Crowley," Ordo Templi Orientis, 2015. The Hermetic Library. http://hermetic.com/crowley /confessions/chapter10.html.

Cornelius, J. Edward. *Aleister Crowley and the Ouija Board*. Port Townsend, WA: Feral House, 2005.

Cornell, James. *The Monster of Loch Ness*. New York: Scholastic Book Services, 1977.

Costello, Peter. *In Search of Lake Monsters*. San Antonio, TX: Anomalist Books, 2002.

Crowe, Cameron. "The Durable Led Zeppelin: A Conversation with Jimmy Page and Robert Plant." *Rolling Stone*, March 13, 1975.

Crowley, Aleister. *The Confessions of Aleister Crowley: An Autohagiography*. London: Penguin Classics, 1989.

———. "The Magician of Loch Ness: Uncanny Happenings at Manor of Boleskine." *Empire News*, November 12, 1933.

———. *Moonchild*. Boston: Weiser Books, 2002.

"Culloden Ghosts." About Aberdeen. http://www.aboutaberdeen .com/culloden-ghosts.php. Accessed 2015.

"Death of a Warlock." *Inverness Courier*, October 16, 1833.

"Death Mills (1945)." IMDb.com. http://www.imdb.com/title /tt0259271/plotsummary?ref_=tt_ov_pl. Accessed 2015.

Devereux, Paul. "Paul Devereux Speaking at the Rollright Stones: Part 1, The Dragon Project" (transcript). The Megalith Portal. http://www.megalithic.co.uk/mm/book/devereux1trans.htm. Accessed 2015.

Dieckhoff, Cyril H. "Mythological Beings in Gaelic Folklore." *Transactions of the Gaelic Society of Inverness* 29 (1914–19).

Dinsdale, Angus. *The Man Who Filmed Nessie: Tim Dinsdale and the Enigma of Loch Ness*. Surrey, Canada: Hancock House Publishers, 2013.

Dinsdale, Tim. *The Leviathans*. London: Futura Publications, 1976.

———. *Loch Ness Monster*, 4th ed. London: Routledge & Kegan, 1976.

———. *The Story of the Loch Ness Monster*. London: Target, 1977.

"A Diver's Experience." *Northern Chronicle*, January 31, 1934.

Downes, Corinna. "Where do we go from here/is it down to the lake I fear?" Still On the Track: The Voice of the International Zoological Community, September 21, 2009. http:// forteanzoology.blogspot.com/2009/09/corinna-downes -where-do-we-go-from.html.

Downes, Jonathan. *Monster Hunter*. Woolsery, UK: CFZ Press, 2004.

———. *Monster of the Mere*. Woolsery, UK: CFZ Press, 2002.

Editors of Encyclopedia Britannica. "Saint Adamnan: Irish Abbot and Scholar." http://www.britannica.com/biography /Saint-Adamnan. Accessed 2015.

Erika. "Could Nessie Be a Giant Salamander?" Weird Animal Report, January 22, 2013. http://weirdanimalreport.com/article /could-nessie-be-giant-salamander.

"The Evidence: Index of Land Based Monster Sightings." Legend of Nessie, 2009. http://www.nessie.co.uk/htm/the_evidence /sight2.html.

"Filey Brigg." Mysterious Britain & Ireland. http://www .mysteriousbritain.co.uk/england/north-yorkshire/legends /filey-brigg.html. Accessed 2015.

"The Filey Dragon: Or Things that Go Bump in the Bay." Fileybay .com. http://www.fileybay.com/dragon/index.html. Accessed 2015.

Fleming, Maureen, and Virginia King. *The Loch Ness Monster Mystery*. Hawthorn, Australia: Mimosa Publications Ltd., 1995.

"Forestry Commission Scotland—Queen's View." Highland Perthshire. http://www.highlandperthshire.org/allnature -wildlife/nwpitlochry/1655-Forestry-Commission-Scotland -Queens-View. Accessed 2015.

Forrest, Richard. "A Few Reasons Why the Loch Ness Monster Is Not a Plesiosaur." The Plesiosaur Site, January 28, 2014. http:// plesiosaur.com/lochness.php.

———. "The Plesiosaur Site." The Plesiosaur Site, February 1, 2014. http://plesiosaur.com.

Fortean Slip. "Loch Ness Monster Classic Sighting Account Mr. And Mrs. George Spicer." YouTube, published February 23, 2015. https://www.youtube.com/watch?v=2W58v-v8Ofw.

Freeman, Richard. *Dragons: More Than a Myth?* Woolsery, UK: CFZ Press, 2005.

———. "Welsh Dragons." The Spooky Isles, July 25, 2014. http://www.spookyisles.com/2014/07/welsh-dragons-everything-you-need-to-know.

"F. W. Holiday and the Loch Ness terror." All About Heaven. http://www.allaboutheaven.org/observations/8707/221/f-w-holiday-and-the-loch-ness-terror-010851. Accessed 2015.

Gallman, Brett. "Psychomania (1973)." Oh, the Horror!, October 25, 2009. http://www.oh-the-horror.com/page.php?id=564.

Godfrey, Linda. *Real Wolfmen.* New York: Tarcher, 2012.

Gordon, Seton. *A Highland Year.* London: Eyre & Spottiswoode, 1944.

Gould, Charles. *Dragons, Unicorns, and Sea Serpents.* Mineola, NY: Dover Publications, Inc., 2002.

Gould, Rupert T. *The Loch Ness Monster.* Secaucus, NJ: Citadel Press, 1976.

"The Gwyber/Wyvern of Coed y Moch." Nannau.com. http://nannau.com/folklore/wyvern-of-coed-y-moch.php. Accessed 2015.

Hallowell, Michael J. *The House That Jack Built.* Stroud, UK: Amberley Publishing, 2008.

Halpenny, Bruce Barrymore. *Ghost Stations IV: True Ghost Stories.* Durham, UK: Casdec, 1991.

Handel, Peter. H, qtd. in "Periodically I hear stories about ball lightning. Does this phenomenon really exist?" *Scientific*

American, July 18, 1987. http://www.scientificamerican.com /article/periodically-i-hear-stori.

Hapgood, Sarah. "Loch Ness—Area of High Strangeness Indeed." sjhstrangetales blog, June 20, 2011. https://sjhstrangetales .wordpress.com/2011/06/20/loch-ness-area-of-high -strangeness-indeed.

Harpur, Merrily. *Mystery Big Cats*. Loughborough, UK: Heart of Albion Press, 2006.

Henderson, William T. *Notes on the Folk-Lore of the Northern Counties of England and the Borders*. Lenox, MA: HardPress Publishing, 2012.

Herbert, Dean. "Alert as UFO Is Sighted Over Loch Ness." *Express*, August 22, 2011. http://www.express.co.uk/news.uk/266478 /Alert-as-UFO-is-sighted-over-Loch-Ness.

Holiday, F. W. *The Dragon and the Disc*. New York: Norton, 1973.

————."Exorcism and UFO Landin at Loch Ness." *Flying Saucer Review*, Vol. 19, Issue 5, September–October 1973.

————. *The Great Orm of Loch Ness*. New York: Norton, 1969.

Holiday, Ted. *The Goblin Universe*. Woodbury, MN: Llewelyn Publications, 1986.

Hymenaeus Beta XII°. "Aleister Crowley." US Grand Lodge: Ordo Templi Orientis, 2015. http://oto-usa.org/thelema/crowley.

"Inverness Man Reports Puma-Like Sighting." *Nessie's Loch Ness Times*. September 8, 2001. http://www.thefrasers.com/nessie /news/nesspapro90801.html.

Jeffrey, Martin. "The Big Hairy Encounter," February 1998. http:// homepage.ntlworld.com/chris.mullins/DERBYSHIRE%20 BHM.htm.

"John Dee—Astrologer to the Queen." http://www .bibliotecapleyades.net/bb/john_dee.htm. Accessed 2015.

Johnson, Ben. "The Kelpie." Historic UK. http://www.historic-uk.com/CultureUK/The-Kelpie. Accessed 2015.

Johnstone, Christian Isobel. *Clan-Albin: A National Tale.* Vol. I. Edinburgh, UK: John Moir, 1815.

Jones, Josh. "Aleister Crowley: *The Wickedest Man in the World* Documents the Life of the Bizarre Occultist, Poet & Mountaineer." Open Culture, March 20, 2014. http://www.openculture.com/2014/03/aleister-crowley-the-wickedest-man-in-the-world.html.

Keating, Kevin. "Did Navy Use Fish Story As Cloak? Pend Oreille Paddler Said To Be Subs." *The Spokesman-Review*, November 15, 1996. http://m.spokesman.com/stories/1996/nov/15/did-navy-use-fish-story-as-cloak-pend-oreille.

"Kelpie." Mythical Creatures Guide, Jun 10 2013. http://www.mythicalcreaturesguide.com/page/Kelpie.

Kirk, John. *In the Domain of Lake Monsters.* Toronto, Canada: Key Porter Books, Ltd., 1998.

Lee, Paul. "About Dr. John Dee." JohnDee.org, September 1, 1996. http://www.johndee.org/DEE.html.

"The Linton Worm." ScotClans. http://www.scotclans.com/scotland/scottish-myths/scottish-monsters/linton-worm. Accessed 2015.

"Loch Morar Monster Morag Sightings Uncovered." BBC News, February 25, 2013. http://www.bbc.com/news/uk-scotland-highlands-islands-21574832.

"Operation Cleansweep and the High Priest of British Witchcaft —the 'Loch Ness Battle of the Broomsticks'!!!" http://www.lochness.co.uk/witches. Accessed 2015.

"The Each Uisge (Water Horse)." LochNessWater. http://www
.lochnesswater.co.uk/nessie_monster_mythology.htm.
Accessed 2015.

"Lustleigh Cleave Ghosts." Legendary Dartmoor, March 25, 2016.
http://www.legendarydartmoor.co.uk/ancients_cleave.htm.

Lyons, Gordon. "Vickers Wellington N2980: Loch Ness Highland." Air Crash Sites Scotland. http://www.aircrashsites
-scotland.co.uk/wellington_loch-ness.htm. Accessed 2015.

MacDonald, Alexander. *Story and Song from Loch Ness-Side*. Inverness, UK: Gaelic Society of Inverness, 1982.

Mackal, Roy P. *The Monsters of Loch Ness*. Chicago: The Swallow
Press, Inc., 1980.

Mackinlay, James M. *Folklore of Scottish Lochs and Springs*. White-
fish, MT: Kessinger Publishing, LLC, 2004.

Macleod, Calum. "Big Cat Sighting Sparks Lambing Time Farm
Alert." *Inverness Courier*, May 2, 2000.

Marrs, Jim. *Psi Spies*. Wayne, NJ: New Page Books, 2007.

"Marsden Grotto, South Shields." Haunted Rooms. http://www
.hauntedrooms.co.uk/product/marsden-grotto. Accessed 2015.

Martin, David M., and Alastair Boyd. *Nessie: The Surgeon's Photograph Exposed*. London: Books For Dillons Only, 1999.

Matrix. "Irish Myths and Legends." Vagabond, January 9, 2015.
http://vagabondtoursofireland.ie/irish-myths-legends.

Matthews, Marcus. *Big Cats Loose in Britain*. Woolsery, UK: CFZ
Press, 2007.

McCarthy, Michael. "Cold, Wet Winter Blamed for Cliff Collapse
at Beachy Head." *Independent*, April 4, 2001. http://www
.independent.co.uk/environment/cold-wet-winter-blamed
-for-cliff-collapse-at-beachy-head-5364799.html.

McConville, Ben. "Nessie Caught on Tape? You Decide." Science on NBCnews.com, June 1, 2007. http://www.nbcnews.com /id/18970301/ns/technology_and_science-science/t/nessie -caught-tape-you-decide/#.Vd86hpeILoY.

Meredith, Dennis L. *Search at Loch Ness.* New York: Quadrangle, 1977.

Merton, Reginald. "Edward Kelly and John Dee." Alchemylab .com. http://www.alchemylab.com/kellydee.htm. Accessed 2015.

"Morag." Unknown Explorers, 2006. http://www.unknown explorers.com/morag.php.

Morrison, Jenny. "Meet the Real Monster of Loch Ness." *Scotland Now,* May 25, 2014. http://www.scotlandnow.dailyrecord /co.uk/lifestyle/heritage/meet-real-monster-loch-ness -3594704.

"Mystery Monster Spotted in the River Nene at Whittlesey." *Bexhill-on-Sea Observer,* June 19, 2015. http://www .bexhillobserver.net/news/local/mystery-monster-spotted -in-the-river-nene-at-whittlesey-1-6808344.

Naish, Darren. "The Loch Ness Monster Seen on Land." Science Blogs, October 2, 2009. http://scienceblogs.com /tetrapodzoology/2009/10/02/loch-ness-monster-on-land.

———. "Photos of the Loch Ness Monster, Revisited." *Scientific American,* July 10, 2013. http://blogs.scientificamerican.com /tetrapod-zoology/photos-of-the-loch-ness-monster-revisited.

"Nessie Filmed by Scientist?" s8int.com. http://s8int.com/phile /dino42.html. Accessed 2015.

"The Nessie Hunters: Dr. Robert Rines." Legend of Nessie, 2009. http://www.nessie.co.uk/htm/the_nessie_hunters/hunter1 .html.

Newkirk, Greg. "Aleister Crowley and the Unfinished Boleskine House Ritual: Loch Ness' Other, Stranger Monster." Week In Weird, April 11, 2011. http://weekinweird.com/2011/04/11/the-boleskine-house-loch-ness-other-stranger-monster.

Nicholl, Charles. "The Last Days of Edward Kelley, Alchemist to the Emperor." London Review of Books, April 19, 2001. http://www.lrb.co.uk/v23/n08/charles-nicholl/the-last-years-of-edward-kelley-alchemist-to-the-emperor.

Nicholson, Edward Williams Byron. Golspie: Contributions to its Folklore. London: David Nutt, 1897.

An Ode on the Popular Superstitions of the Highlands of Scotland, considered as the subject of poetry. Written by the late Mr William Collins: and communicated to the Royal Society of Edinburgh, by Alexander Carlyle (1788). London: British Library, 2011.

Omand, Donald. Experiences of a Present Day Exorcist. London: William Kimber, 1970.

"Searching for Nessie: Operation Deepscan." Legend of Nessie, 2009. http://www.nessie.co.uk/htm/searching_for_nessie/deepscan.html.

Parkinson, Daniel. "The Linton Worm." Mysterious Britain & Ireland. http://www.mysteriousbritain.co.uk/scotland/roxburghshire/legends/the-linton-worm.html. Accessed 2015.

Plambeck, Steve. "A Beast With Two Backs—The Gray Photo Deconstructed." The Loch Ness Giant Salamander. http://thelochnessgiantsalamander.blogspot.com/2012/08/a-beast-with-two-backs-gray-photo.html. August 28, 2012.

Raynor, Dick. "Alex Campbell." Loch Ness Investigation, 2009. http://www.lochnessinvestigation.com/alexcampbell.htm.

————. "The Flipper Pictures Re-examined." Loch Ness Investigation, May 2009. http://www.lochnessinvestigation.com /flipper.html.

————. "Pumas & Other Big Cats Near Loch Ness." Loch Ness Investigation. http://www.lochnessinvestigation.com/Pumas .html. Accessed 2015.

Redfern, Nick. "The Camel-Horse of Loch Ness." Mysterious Universe, June 16, 2015. http://mysteriousuniverse.org/2015/06 /the-camel-horse-of-loch-ness.

————. Man-Monkey: In Search of the British Bigfoot. Woolsery, UK: CFZ Press, 2007.

Richardson, Alan. Aleister Crowley and Dion Fortune. Woodbury, MN: Llewellyn Publications, 2009.

Rose, David Murray. Letter to the Scotsman, October 20, 1933.

Sanidopoulos, John. "Saint Columba and the Loch Ness Monster." Mystagogy Resource Center, November 12, 2010. http://www .johnsanidopoulos.com/2010/11/saint-columba-and-loch-ness -monster.html.

"A Scene at Lochend." Inverness Courier, July 1, 1852.

"Scotland's Forgotten Cat; Fewer than 100 Remain ..." Save the Scottish Wildcat, 2014. http://www.scottishwildcats.co.uk.

Selwyn-Holmes, Alex. "Doc Shiels." Iconic Photos, July 19, 2009. https://iconicphotos.wordpress.com/tag/doc-shiels.

Shiels, Tony "Doc." Monstrum! A Wizard's Tale. Woolsery, UK: CFZ Press, 2011.

Shuker, Dr. Karl P. N. "Does the Loch Ness Monster Have a Split Personality? Revealing Nessie's Strangest Identities." Shuker Nature, July 16, 2013. http://karlshuker.blogspot.com /2013/07/does-loch-ness-monster-have-split.html.

———. *Dragons in Zoology, Cryptozoology, and Culture.* Greenville, OH: Coachwhip Publications, 2013.

Spence, Richard B. *Secret Agent 666, Aleister Crowley, British Intelligence and the Occult.* Port Townsend, WA: Feral House, 2008.

Speigel, Lee. "Mystery of Loch Ness UFO Photo Deepens." *The Huffington Post,* July 1, 2015. http://www.huffingtonpost.com/2015/07/01/loch-ness-ufo-photo-debunked_n_7675456.html.

———. "UFOs Spotted Above Loch Ness." *The Huffington Post,* June 17, 2015. http://www.huffingtonpost.com/2015/06/13/tourist-photographs-loch-ness-ufos_n_7554206.html.

"St. Columba." Catholic Online, 2016. http://www.catholic.org/saints/saint.php?saint_id=419.

Stewart, W. Grant. *The Popular Superstitions and Festive Amusements of the Highlanders of Scotland.* London: Aylott & Jones, 1851.

Stott, Colin. *Four-Teans go to Ness.* Self published, 2009.

"A Strange Fish in Loch Ness." *Inverness Courier,* October 8, 1868.

Suster, Gerald. *The Legacy of the Beast, the Life Work and Influence of Aleister Crowley.* York Beach, ME: Samuel Weiser, Inc., 1989.

"Terror of the Zygons." BBC. http://www.bbc.co.uk/doctorwho/classic/episodeguide/terrorzygons/detail.shtml. Accessed 2015.

"Tiamat." Mythical-Folk. http://www.themystica.com/mythical-folk/~articles/t/tiamat.html. Accessed 2015.

"Tiamat: Lady of Primeval Chaos, the Great Mother of the Gods of Babylon." Gateways to Babylon. http://www.gatewaystobabylon.com/gods/ladies/ladytiamat.html. Accessed 2015.

"Tim Dinsdale. Loch Ness. 1960." YouTube, published October 8, 2013. https://www.youtube.com/watch?v=GdQUbLKwCvQ.

Vitimus, Andrieh. *Hands-On Chaos Magic: Reality Manipulation Through the Ovayki Current*. Woodbury, MN: Llewellyn, 2009.

Watson, Roland. "Analysis of the Peter MacNab Photograph." Loch Ness Monster, February 19, 2012. http://lochnessmystery .blogspot.com/2012/02/analysis-of-peter-macnab-photograph .html.

———. "The Hugh Gray Photograph Revisited." Loch Ness Monster, June 26, 2011. http://lochnessmystery.blogspot .com/2011/06/hugh-gray-photograph-revisited_26.html.

———. "The Lachlan Stuart Photograph (Part 1)." Loch Ness Monster, July 22, 2012. http://lochnessmystery.blogspot .com/2012/07/the-lachlan-stuart-photograph-part-1.html.

———. "The Lachlan Stuart Photograph (Part 4). Loch Ness Monster, January 3, 2013. http://lochnessmystery.blogspot .com/2013/01/the-lachlan-stuart-photograph-part-four.html.

———. "New Theory on the Hugh Gray Photograph." Loch Ness Monster, September 5, 2012. http://lochnessmystery.blogspot .com/2012/09/new-theory-on-hugh-gray-photograph.html.

———. "Tim Dinsdale, Nessie and the Paranormal." Loch Ness Monster, September 18, 2012. http://lochnessmystery.blogspot .com/2012/09/tim-dinsdale-nessie-and-paranormal.html.

———. *The Water Horses of Loch Ness*. CreateSpace Independent Publishing Platform, 2011.

Webb, Sam. "UFO Spotted Over Loch Ness: Mystery Craft 'Seen Hovering Above Famous Scottish Tourist Spot.'" *Mirror*, June 10, 2015. http://www.mirror.co.uk/news/uk-news/ufo-spotted -over-loch-ness-5855773.

"The Wellington Bomber and Loch Ness." Loch Ness Water. http://www.lochnesswater.co.uk/crashed_ww2_bombers.htm. Accessed 2015.

"A White Witch Returns to Loch Ness." STVNews. http://news
.stv.tv/scotland/76515-white-witch-returns-to-loch-ness.
Accessed 2015.

"White Witch to Tempt Nessie." BBC News, June 11, 2003. http://
news.bbc.co.uk/2/hi/uk_news/england/southern_counties
/2981386.stm.

Whyte, Constance. *More Than a Legend, The Story of the Loch Ness
Monster.* London: Hamish Hamilton, 1961.

Wilford, John Noble. "Probers Miss Nessie, Find New Stonehenge." *Chicago Tribune*, December 12, 1976.

Williams, Rhiannon. "'Best Ever' Photograph of Loch Ness Monster Revealed as a Fake." *The Telegraph*, October 4, 2013. http://
www.telegraph.co.uk/news/newstopics/howaboutthat
/10355915/Best-ever-photograph-of-Loch-Ness-monster
-revealed-as-a-fake.html.

Wilson, Colin. *Aleister Crowley: The Nature of the Beast.* Wellingbor-
ough, UK: Aquarian Press, 1987.

"Witch Casts Spell to Protect Nessie." *Daily Mail.* http://www
.dailymail.co.uk/news/article-40704/Witch-casts-spell-protect
-Nessie.html. Accessed 2015.

Witchell, Nicholas. *The Loch Ness Story.* London: Corgi Books,
1982.

Zarzynski, Joseph W. *Monster Wrecks of Loch Ness and Lake Champlain.* Wilton, NY: M-Z Information, 1986.

To Write to the Author

If you wish to contact the author or would like more information about this book, please write to the author in care of Llewellyn Worldwide Ltd. and we will forward your request. Both the author and publisher appreciate hearing from you and learning of your enjoyment of this book and how it has helped you. Llewellyn Worldwide Ltd. cannot guarantee that every letter written to the author can be answered, but all will be forwarded. Please write to:

Nick Redfern
⅟ Llewellyn Worldwide
2143 Wooddale Drive
Woodbury, MN 55125-2989
Please enclose a self-addressed stamped envelope for reply,
or $1.00 to cover costs. If outside the U.S.A., enclose
an international postal reply coupon.

Many of Llewellyn's authors have websites with additional information and resources. For more information, please visit our website at http://www.llewellyn.com.

Chupacabra Road Trip
In Search of the Elusive Beast
NICK REDFERN

In 1995, Puerto Rico was seized with mass hysteria over a new menace lurking in the rainforests, gruesomely killing livestock, leaving strange holes in their necks, and draining their bodies of blood. Described by eyewitnesses as a devilish creature three feet tall with spikes along its back and a mouth full of razor-sharp fangs, the strange animal was given the name Chupacabra—Spanish for "goat-sucker."

Join noted monster hunter Nick Redfern and his spirited crew as they traverse the rugged backcountry of Puerto Rico, Mexico, and Texas investigating the continuing legacy of this fearsome beast. Whether he's interviewing locals, analyzing physical evidence, or sorting out the facts from the legends, Nick's journey into the realm of the Chupacabra will make you wonder just what's out there lurking in the night.

978-0-7387-4448-3, 264 pp., 5 ³⁄₁₆ x 8   **$15.99**

EXPLORING THE MYTH & DISCOVERING THE TRUTH

BIGFOOT

TOM BURNETTE & ROB RIGGS

Bigfoot
Exploring the Myth & Discovering the Truth
Tom Burnette and Rob Riggs

Over the past twenty years, two men from different parts of the United States have followed and developed a friendly connection with the mysterious ape-like creature known as Bigfoot. Now, with forty-plus years of combined field study, these experienced investigators present a detailed collection of personal stories, ethnographic research, and theories surrounding the Bigfoot legend.

Join authors Rob Riggs and Tom Burnette, whose many years of commitment to the search and dedicated study reveal their true encounters with the elusive, wild being. Explore the history, habitats, and more in this collection of substantial evidence of Bigfoot's existence and thought-provoking discussions for continued research. From the possibility of having psychic powers to why it's so hard to find, *Bigfoot* goes beyond the myth to the reality of this amazing ape-man.

978-0-7387-3631-0, 264 pp., 5 ³⁄₁₆ x 8 **$15.99**

KEN GERHARD

Foreword by Dr. Karl P. N. Shuker

ENCOUNTERS WITH FLYING

HUMANOIDS

mothman, manbirds, gargoyles & other winged beasts

Encounters with Flying Humanoids
Mothman, Manbirds, Gargoyles
& Other Winged Beasts
KEN GERHARD

A strange creature with gigantic, blood-red embers for eyes crept out of the dark in West Virginia. Dozens of witnesses reported seeing the winged beast—later identified as the Mothman—take flight, chasing cars at speeds exceeding 100 miles per hour.

Cryptozoologist Ken Gerhard has traveled the world collecting evidence on the Mothman, the Owlman, the Van Meter Creature, the Valkyrie of Voltana, the Houston Batman, and other strange "bird people" that have been sighted throughout history. Packed with famous historical cases and dozens of chilling first-person accounts, this is the first book to focus exclusively on flying humanoids—a wide array of airborne entities that seem to "feed off our fear like psychic vampires."

978-0-7387-3720-1, 240 pp., 5 ³⁄₁₆ x 8   **$14.99**

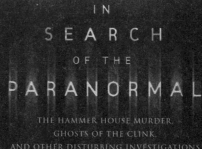

IN
SEARCH
OF THE
PARANORMAL

THE HAMMER HOUSE MURDER,
GHOSTS OF THE CLINK,
AND OTHER DISTURBING INVESTIGATIONS

RICHARD ESTEP

In Search of the Paranormal
The Hammer House Murder, Ghosts of the Clink, and Other Disturbing Investigations
RICHARD ESTEP

From exploring the Tower of London to investigating a haunted Colorado firehouse, paranormal researcher Richard Estep takes you behind the scenes for an up-close-and-personal encounter with a fascinating legion of hauntings. This collection reveals some of the most chilling, captivating, and weird cases that Richard has investigated over the past twenty years, in England and in the United States.

In Search of the Paranormal is filled with rich historical detail, present-day research, and compelling eyewitness accounts. You are there with the team at each haunted location: walking through a desecrated graveyard, shivering in a dark basement, getting thrown into The Clink, watching a "ghost-lit" stage in an old theater. Employing a variety of investigative methods—from high-tech gadgets to old-fashioned practices such as dowsing, table tipping, and Ouija boards—Richard Estep and his team uncover the dark mysteries of the paranormal realm.

978-0-7387-4488-9, 264 pp., 5 ³⁄₁₆ x 8   **$15.99**

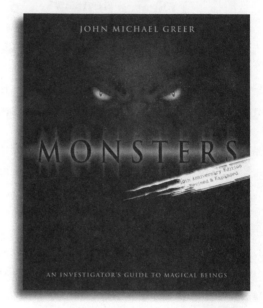

JOHN MICHAEL GREER

MONSTERS

10th Anniversary Edition
Revised & Expanded

AN INVESTIGATOR'S GUIDE TO MAGICAL BEINGS

Monsters
An Investigator's Guide to Magical Beings
JOHN MICHAEL GREER

Of course that monster hiding under your bed when you were little didn't really exist. Vampires, werewolves, zombies, demons —they're simply figments of our imagination, right? After all, their existence has never been scientifically proven. But there is one giant problem with such an easy dismissal of these creepy creatures: people keep encountering them.

Join occult scholar John Michael Greer for a harrowing journey into the reality of the impossible. Combining folklore, Western magical philosophy, and actual field experience, *Monsters: An Investigator's Guide to Magical Beings* is required reading for both active and armchair monster hunters.

This tenth anniversary edition of the quintessential guide to magical beings features a new preface, new chapters on chimeras and zombies, and updates on werewolves, dragons, and the fae.

978-0-7387-0050-2, 312 pp., 7 ½ x 9 ⅛   **$19.95**
